before the latest date sta___

KT-470-915

My Da____
GUV'NOR

My Dad THE GUV'NOR

The true story of my life with the legendary
hard man, Lenny McLean

Kelly McLean

With Lee Wortley

JOHN BLAKE

Published by John Blake Publishing,
2.25, The Plaza,
535 Kings Road,
Chelsea Harbour
London, SW10 0SZ

www.johnblakebooks.com

www.facebook.com/johnblakebooks ⬛
twitter.com/jblakebooks ⬛

This edition first published in 2018

ISBN: 978 1 78606 919 1

British Library Cataloguing-in-Publication Data:

A catalogue record for this book is available from the British Library.

Design by www.envydesign.co.uk

Printed and bound in Great Britain by Clays Ltd, Elcograf S.p.A.

1 3 5 7 9 10 8 6 4 2

Papers used by John Blake Publishing are natural, recyclable products made from wood grown in sustainable forests. The manufacturing processes conform to the environmental regulations of the country of origin.

Every attempt has been made to contact the relevant copyright-holders, but some were unobtainable. We would be grateful if the appropriate people could contact us.

John Blake Publishing is an imprint of Bonnier Publishing
www.bonnierpublishing.com

CONTENTS

FOREWORD

A letter from my partner, Scott Richardson

I have always had a weakness for redheads. My friend told me there was a redhead, 'good-looking, running this bar on the Mile End Road. She works the lunchtime shift.' I thought to myself I should go and take a look, see for myself what he was talking about. So I made arrangements to meet him. As I entered the pub, I was immediately on it: she had the long red hair, it was a win–win situation for me.

She knew exactly what people drank. I didn't waste any time introducing myself; I offered to buy her a drink, which I must say she declined. I was impressed by the way she came across –

you could have a laugh with her, but she knew when and how to cut it dead if it was going too far. When people have a drink it can lower their morals and they can try to push things a bit too far and cross the line. But Kelly would have none of it. Looking back, no one took a liberty. She pulled everyone together; she was the conductor in the middle and she was directing all of us.

For the next six months I was in that bar every day at midday, and at ten past she would walk in as if she owned the place. I'm not sure if it was my good looks that did it – probably not, I was just persistent – but eventually I wore her down and Kelly agreed to go out for something to eat. I went round her flat to pick her up. I waited and waited and waited – 'I'll be five minutes, I'm nearly ready.' I should have known the drill because of her timekeeping down the pub.

The wait was worth it: she looked stunning. You can judge how a night is going – one minute it's seven o'clock and then it's midnight and the restaurant staff are cleaning up around you.

Helping Kelly write her book has made me realise how much your childhood shapes the person you become. It has made me think how I never saw the signs that Kelly had many emotional issues, issues that she has kept hidden from the world. A lot of stuff she has put to the back of her mind and just blocked it all out. These issues would surface every now and then and it would all get on top of her, and in my view she would drift into depression or, as she calls it, 'a low period'.

Val, Kelly's mum, always liked to throw parties. Only a close circle of friends and family was invited. One thing someone asked me at one of Val's parties, something that has always stuck in my mind, was 'Do you find Kelly childish?' That question is imbedded in my brain. Every now and then it comes into my thoughts. I try and work out where they were coming from. I should have addressed it there and then, but I didn't.

The knowledge I have is of Kelly, Val and what Kelly has told me about her dad. It's unfair to say Kelly is childish – I believe she was never given the tools through her childhood and early adult years to deal with certain issues that an adult has to address. Whatever problem she had, she would rely on her mum and dad to sort out. That's not a bad thing, it's part of being a parent and I would be the same if my child needed help. Maybe more communication between them would have made her take more responsibility for her actions. Instead, money would get thrown at the problem or she would shut herself away and block it out, leave it for someone else to deal with and dismiss it. Everyone close to her, including myself, would just paper over the cracks. We would never get to the root of the problem; it would simply go away, but six months later, it would surface again. We would go through the same process over and over again. The impact does not only affect her, it affects the whole dynamics of the family. Kelly is working hard to try and see the signs that start this process off, but there is still a long way to go. I think telling her story in this book will help in her recovery.

Kelly, from what I gather, is very much like her dad: she flies off the handle at the drop of a hat. The only difference is that he was nineteen stone, a big powerful man! Their minds would process something in the same way. Both would get frustrated with the world because no one else saw it the way they did. Like being an alcoholic or a drug addict, unless they have the illness themselves, people never really understand it fully: why someone is like they are, what is going through their head.

FOREWORD

As I got to know Kelly, I realised there was a lot more to her than I was first drawn to. The Kelly most people know likes to be the centre of attention, likes a laugh and can talk for England. She is very much an open book on certain things, but there's a lot of stuff kept locked away in her head that she doesn't tell anybody. If Kelly lets you in the door, you will find there is a soft, caring side, a people-pleaser, someone who will go out of her way to help out a friend in need, someone who wants to be liked and who lacks confidence but puts up a front. Kelly can be misunderstood by some people because of her upfront views – if she has something to say, like it or not, she will tell you how she feels. Most things in her mind are black or white. Once she has said what she has to say, she will move on.

Kelly is a person who is very creative, a person who has tremendous highs but also takes things to heart and can have massive lows as well. There have been good times and bad in our relationship, more good than bad. The bads were extremely bad, and as Kelly herself has written in this book, the truth is that it would have been a lot easier for me to walk away than stay. I never knew how much she relied on Val until her mum died. Only in helping Kelly write this book have I got the answers: why she was such a troubled soul, the secrets she has kept to herself... Listening and talking about her life has helped me understand the complexity of her mind. I now have a better understanding of how it works, the way her thoughts gather pace and how we can stop those thoughts in their tracks.

For many of the fifteen years Kelly and I have been together, I have not always been the most supportive partner. I never understood mental illness – I just saw it as being weak, not strong enough to cope. Kelly did not get a lot of sympathy from me. I was an old-fashioned man who didn't want to know. I wasn't interested; I was narrow-minded. I suppose I too would be guilty of not addressing the problem, or maybe I just didn't understand it.

Coming from the East End, it's football first, the gym second, pub third and your relationship comes a distant fourth. Luckily, I realised I had got my priorities in the wrong order before it was too late.

I would not want to live my life without Kelly. We have both got some strange ways but we still laugh and never struggle to make conversation when we go out – well, *she* doesn't! I don't want to get old; it comes to us all though, and I hope when I do, it will be with Kelly by my side.

I am very proud of what she has achieved. I have read her book and there are some sad stories in it, also some stories that will make you laugh out loud. Well done, Kelly! Your mum and dad would be as proud of you as I am.

INTRODUCTION

My name is Kelly Valerie McLean and I think it's time to tell you the real story behind my dad, Lenny McLean, The Guv'nor, in all its highs and lows. As you read this book, you will see how my dad changes from one man to another. I'll begin with my very first memories as a young child and move on to my life as it stands today.

I have seen the overwhelming support for my dad that still exists, with fans still congregating online to talk about him and his legendary bouts. In the last couple of years, I have started a Facebook group dedicated to him, joining forces with Lee Wortley. Lee has run sites and blogs in support of my dad for the past twenty or so years, and at that time was already running a flourishing site called 'Dedicated to Lenny McLean'.

On joining forces, it became immediately apparent that Lee and I needed a new name for our site. Therefore, we thought what better way to accomplish this than to join Lee's name to mine, thus coming up with the obvious 'Dedicated to My Dad, The Guv'nor'.

Along with myself and Lee, we have four administrators: Nikki Baker, Mark Davies, Freddie Tonks and Sue Sillitoe, who with their fantastic help make the site as successful as it is today, with over 6,000 loyal members. We try to make it a friendly community for my dad's fans where they can really connect, and I'm very proud of how well-received it has been.

In just a few months I have received a whole heap of inspirational messages, many of them extremely heartfelt, from people informing me how my dad's bestselling book, *The Guv'nor*, has changed their lives, helping them to deal with their own issues and tackle difficult situations. This alone has been inspiration enough for me.

This book is of course about my dad and the life I shared with him, but the personality found here in this text is written from the heart – with me, what you get is what you see. Like me, my book is a one-hundred-mile-an-hour thrust through time, an in-your-face account of a life that will have your emotions jumping from one extreme to another. If nothing else, life with my father was a once-in-a-lifetime experience.

1

THE EARLY YEARS

I'm known as The Guv'nor's Daughter – I am The
Guv'nor's Daughter. But what does that mean?

I was about six years old and my brother Jamie was
about seven. It was Christmas in the late 1970s, a time
of year that was incredibly special in the McLean
household and remains so for me and my family. We
lived at 51 Allen Road, on the second floor of a block
of flats. The flats were in the heart of the East End of
London, right behind the Roman Road Market.

Back in the sixties and seventies, women in the area
would dress up to the nines just to go out shopping
for the day. Looking from our window, you could see
many an East End housewife dressed in what looked

like their best outfit with a full face of makeup and more jewellery than I have ever worn in my entire life. It was the costume type, what you might consider as the kind of cheap tat you'd see on every market stall up and down the country. Looking back, it's nice that they at least felt special for the day – I guess that's all that mattered.

Christmas was everything in our house, but it wasn't just about my brother Jamie and me. No, it was as much about the big guy himself, The Guv'nor. My dad was the biggest kid of all. Perhaps this was because, as a child, he didn't get anything and was bullied by his evil stepfather, Jim Irwin. He once broke my dad's ribs, putting him in hospital. Looking back, a huge amount of damage was done during Dad's childhood. Not only physically, but mentally, as a result of what he saw, heard and learnt as a child, thinking the behaviour he'd witnessed from that man was quite normal.

That Christmas morning, Jamie and I got up and went upstairs to the front room. Our flat was unconventional; you had to go upstairs to the front room. As I remember, we had warm air heating which came out of a duct. The heating was only upstairs, and because heat rises, the downstairs bedrooms were always freezing in winter. The front room ceiling was covered in Christmas decorations. I loved them because they disguised the deep yellow nicotine stains, a by-product of my parents' heavy smoking. This nasty habit they shared would eventually kill the pair of them.

In our house, we always had a real Christmas tree, but unlike the real trees of today, back then, by the time Christmas Day came, our tree was as bald as a f**king badger! All of the pine needles would be scattered across the floor. As it turned out, on this particular Christmas morning, the pine needles were the only things that were on the floor, because for some strange reason, there was not a Christmas present to be seen. My brother and I were in turmoil. Immediately, we ran down the stairs into our parents' room. Angry and disappointed, we were shouting, 'Mum, Dad, Father Christmas hasn't been! He hasn't left us any presents at all!'

'Wait a minute,' my dad shouted, 'I can hear him. Just get into bed with Mummy and I will help him. He's probably just running late!'

I still laugh to myself, thinking about it now.

Within a few seconds, we could hear lots of commotion as Dad was obviously running up and down the stairs, huffing and puffing, 'F**k this, f**k that!' All of a sudden, and much to our delight, he opened the door and said, 'Come on, kids, HE'S BEEN!' As quickly as our little legs could carry us, we ran upstairs, and there, to our amazement, were what seemed to be millions and millions of presents. It was like Santa's Grotto up there, and if I cast my mind's eye back to that Christmas morning, I just have to say our living room looked like the third floor of Hamleys on their busiest day of the year!

Leading up to that Christmas, I had asked for a playhouse. Well, I didn't just get one playhouse, I got three of them instead! I thought I was the Queen of Sheba. My brother Jamie had wanted a snooker table. When you're seven years old, you'd expect to get something like a four-foot snooker table. Well, you would in any normal house, but no, not in our house with The Guv'nor and his Christmas spending spree. Instead, my dad had got Jamie the biggest snooker table you have ever seen!

So, imagine this massive great snooker table in a council maisonette. When my mum set it up in Jamie's bedroom, it fitted snugly in there, but Jamie himself could not. To get into bed, he had to crawl under the snooker table and up over the other side. Imagine how it was for him, trying to play a game of snooker. Looking back it is clear to see that my mum, and especially dad, were showering us with the gifts that they never were given as children. I guess a lot of people from that generation were exactly the same.

As we grew older, Christmas was more to do with my dad. As I said previously, Dad was like a big kid. We had to hide all his presents in our neighbour's house otherwise he would simply turn the house upside down and inside out, looking for them. However, as soon as he had opened them, he would go missing for a few hours, trying every bit of his new clobber on. He would be in his bedroom, in front of the full-length mirror, in nothing but his underpants. You could hear him in there as he was trying everything on. He would sing at the top of his voice, lungs almost bursting, as he belted out the hits of Elvis Presley, Patsy Cline, Frank Sinatra, the lot – oh, and a cheeky little impression of John Wayne, just to give his lungs, and our ears, a rest.

It was the same every Christmas in the McLean family home, right up until our last Christmas before Dad died. Our dad was like Santa with an attitude, bless him!

2

THE SEVENTIES AND EARLY EIGHTIES

The seventies and early eighties were fantastic for my brother Jamie and me. He and I were treated like royalty, and every single person on our manor (estate) made a fuss of us. However, there were the odd few who would take liberties and taunt us and try and pick a fight, simply because of who our dad was.

As young as Jamie and I were, we had a reputation to live up to, because after all, we were Lenny 'The Guv'nor' McLean's kids. My mum had many stories to tell, but the one that always comes leaping to mind is this one…

I was out playing with my friend Tanya Corson (sadly, she has recently passed away – God bless her). Tanya was a very dear friend to me, as was her mum to mine. Anyway, my mum was having her lunch when there was a knock at the door. As she opened it, one of our neighbours was standing there: 'I think Kelly might need you. I've just seen a few girls approach her in the park, and they were all shouting at her,' to which Mum replied, 'Kelly's her father's daughter, she will be fine. I'm going to finish my lunch now. Shut the door on your way out.' The neighbour left with her jaw touching the floor. You see, Mum knew I would be OK and she was right: I was my dad's daughter alright, with the flame-red hair and the red-hot temper to go with it…

Soon after, Mum found me with this bunch of girls, and yes, her intuition was right, because I was the only girl left standing! She was always right on the money where her husband and kids were concerned.

Coincidentally, my dad had one of his unlicensed fights organised for that evening. As he was getting himself hyped up before the fight, Jamie and I were dancing around him and getting under his feet. He lifted us both up so that we hung off each arm, just like dumbbells. We loved it! You see, growing up in our house was far from normal. It also says a lot about our dad that a couple of hours away from a fight, he was mucking about with his kids like that.

Just before Dad left for his fight, Mum was making

tea. Dad shouted, 'Val, order Chinese for about ten o'clock, I won't be long.' True to his word, just as Mum was dishing up the Chinese, he walked into the front room half-cut and began to throw bundles of cash into the air. It felt like we were in a movie. As kids, we had never seen so much money in our lives. It was falling all around us and it felt as if it was in slow motion. Jamie and I were totally mesmerised. I remember catching it all and stuffing it under my pillow – I loved it! My excitement was very short-lived though, because the next morning, once Dad had sobered up, he shouted out, 'Val, where's all my money?' to which my mum hollered back, 'I don't know! Ask the bloody kids, Len!' As you can see, Jamie and I were spoilt rotten and had absolutely everything we could have wanted growing up. Mum and The Guv'nor made sure that, from childhood onwards through to adulthood, we had the best of everything.

My dad always said that I had the memory of an elephant. I can remember being ever so young when some men asked him, did he fancy doing a bank job? Now Dad was not into anything like that at all, and anyone who was close to him would know that, but never wanting to lose face, he said, 'I'm in!' My mum and her best friend Rita said to him at the time, 'Say no, Len, don't do it!' He immediately responded at the top of his voice, 'I have to do it now, do I not? For f**k's sake, I don't need all of this bollocks.'

These men would come round to our house to discuss all the plans – you know, the dos and don'ts, the whys and wherefores. Dad was really up for it in front of them, but as soon as they left the house he was effin' and blindin' at my mum. She just laughed and laughed, seeing him in such a state, and all because he couldn't lose face and say, 'Thanks but no thanks, it's not for me.' My dad hated the thought of anything that could land him in prison; the thought of leaving us killed him.

So, it's the day of the bank job. Mum and her friend Rita are sat there in hysterics while Dad is getting dressed and ready. All of a sudden he shouts, 'F**k this, Rita! What's going on?' We couldn't stop laughing, seeing him with his head stuck down the sleeve of his roll-neck – he was getting himself in a right state. Rita sorted him out and he'd got the roll-neck on properly when the door buzzer went. Mum opened the door and one of the blokes was standing there. He walked in and said to Dad: 'Len it's off, it's not happening, not today.' The look on Dad's face was one of total relief, the colour was starting to come back to his cheeks. 'You are joking, right? I was well hyped up for this. F**k, what a let-down!

Keep me in the loop when it's on,' he said. Luckily, that day never came. Just as well, I think: if it went wrong and there was a police line-up, even if he had his face covered up then I guess he would still have been picked out because of his size.

I have many memories from when I was young. I always had nightmares, which meant that I never slept very well. At night, I used to sit up until quite late with my mum, but as soon as I heard the key go in the door, I would run and hide behind the settee. My dad was a heavy drinker, which was not very nice – both his presence and size were scary enough sober, let alone when he was drunk.

Often Dad would come home boozed-up and start shouting and hollering at Mum. He would be pulling her about and saying things to her that a child really should never have to hear. These incidents made my mum petrified of him; just the sound of his voice would have her quivering. Nevertheless, and I guess the way it was with many men back then, the very next morning, Dad would always be sorry. Not that he remembered much of why he was sorry, I might add.

On one occasion, my dad pulled up in the car outside. You could always hear him way before you caught sight of him, so we always knew when he was home. Mum looked over the balcony and was immediately aware that he was drunk – this was plain for her to see, just by the way his car was parked.

The block of flats we lived in had a set of stairs on either end. Mum came in from looking over the balcony and called to Jamie and I: 'Quick, we're going!'

Every few steps as we were being ushered out of the flats I kept looking back and saying, 'But Mum, what about Lady [our Staffordshire Bull-Terrier]?'

'Lady will be fine, now come on!' said Mum.

We left the flats, and as we were running down one set of stairs, Dad was coming up the other. We all piled into Mum's car and set off, with no idea where we were heading. After what seemed like a long time, we pulled up outside of this building. I remember walking up what seemed at the time to be thousands of stairs – you know how big things seem when you're a kid. Anyway, this building turned out to be a women's refuge in Hackney Road. We sat there for a few hours. Jamie kept crying as he wanted to go home to Dad. Eventually, we left the refuge and Mum said, 'Right, come on kids, your dad will have sobered up by now.' As easy a turnaround as that, it was just one of those things with Dad. For us it was normal – we didn't know any different.

As I have already mentioned, Dad was aggressive enough without drink; his presence alone would make everyone in his vicinity feel like they needed to tread on eggshells. Nothing changed, and through his early twenties, incidents like this were a regular thing. Often, my parents would walk into any busy pub and within a few seconds, the place would immediately begin to empty – everyone was just so terrified of my dad. People would try their best not to make eye contact because Dad would turn at the drop of a hat. No one would dare glance in their direction because he would accuse them of looking at my mum. In those days that would be more than anyone would dare to do. And with Mum being the total opposite of my dad, you can imagine how uncomfortable she would have been. She was just so quiet and reserved, she must have felt so embarrassed.

There was a man on the estate we nicknamed 'the medallion man'. He wore the biggest gold chain round his neck you have ever seen and was built like a brick sh*thouse. One night, Mum and Dad were in a pub and Dad heard medallion man go 'C**t!' Well, that was it, he knocked the fella spark out. No reasons given, no questions asked, just *wallop!* Medallion man fell fast asleep on the floor. Turns out, he had a little holiday at Barts Hospital (St Bartholomew's) for a couple of days.

As you can imagine there were many of these

incidents. Another morning, in the early hours, Dad strolled in. He had barely got out of his coat and he was sick as a dog. Of course Mum had to get up and clean up the mess. She said to my dad, 'Len, what on God's earth have you had to eat that's made you this sick?' He replied, 'I've just bitten some mug's face off!' And with that, he collapsed on his bed.

All of these incidents took their toll and Mum eventually became ill. She was barely eating and rapidly losing weight. She went to the doctor and the advice he gave her was to drink lots of fluids and she'd be fine. Well, that doctor could not have been more off the mark. Very rapidly, Mum's weight dropped from about ten stone to just over six. Eventually, a different doctor referred her to St Clement's Hospital in the East End, a place in those days referred to as a 'mental hospital' (it's no longer there, I might add). St Clement's was a hospital for people suffering with mental illness and depression. Of course this was the kind of action that needed to be taken from day one. Anyway, Mum was in there for a few days. She was diagnosed with anxiety and depression, then given Valium tablets and told to rest up for a couple of days.

We were lost without Mum: she was the family's backbone, and she was our world. Mum's best friend Christine lived next door. She helped us out a lot, especially with my hair, because as you can imagine, The Guv'nor was by no stretch of the imagination a hairdresser. Dad went to visit Mum, although I'm not sure if that helped or hindered her recovery. Jamie and I didn't go, as we were too young to properly understand what was going on. When Mum eventually came home from St Clement's she wanted things to go back to normal. She hated leaving us and she was fed up with Dad's behaviour (the drinking and all of the other goings-on), which was causing the family far too much stress. The pain was obvious to see on her.

Here's a funny little story. Well, not at all funny really, but you'll see what I mean. After a few days of being home, Mum explained to me that Dad 'had a bird'. So, with me being young and naïve at the time, I spent hours searching the house for a bird of the feathered variety, at which point Mum patiently explained, 'No, Kelly, it means Daddy has another woman!' She must have laughed about that for years after. Anyway, as I grew into an adult, I obviously realised what she meant was that Dad had brought some tart home to our house. We found out it was only a one-night stand. Mum knew who it was and I ain't no grass, so I won't name names. Suffice to say, this 'tart' of a woman's daughter is now a very well-known actress.

But Mum had had enough of this type of life and

didn't want it to carry on the way it was, so she gave him an ultimatum: 'Is it the drink or your family? I'm taking the kids to Spain, so while we're away, you need to decide what sort of a life it is that you actually want, Lenny.' So, off to Spain we went, Mum, her sister Debbie, Jamie and me. When we got home, after a fair amount of time away, Dad told Mum: 'You're my world, my family is everything. No more drinking, I promise you, Val.' My parents were never meant to be apart, they were soulmates. It was just a phase for my dad, a selfish phase now dead and buried. As soon as he gave up the drink, life became bearable again. Our little family unit was together again, and happy the way we knew we could be. Also, now I had my proper dad back, life could not have been any better. He was an aggressive character – we didn't know any different – but with drink, he was ten times worse. Therefore, when I say we were happy, I mean we were glad he wasn't drinking.

As a child, I loved cleaning and ironing, but I was a cheeky little thing, and being a flame-headed McLean, I often used this to my advantage. I would say to Mum: 'Mum, if I do the ironing, please could I have the day off school?' To which my sweet and gentle mum would immediately say, 'Yes, Kelly, you can!' The twinkle in her eye showed she was thinking, 'You cheeky little sod!' But hey, that was how my mum's attitude was, all day long...

Brass was all the rage in the seventies and my mum had a lot of ornaments made from it around the house. For hours I would be in my element with a tin of Brasso and a rag. The only problem was Dad – we always had to have an excuse lined up just in case. He was very big on education and hated us missing school. In the mornings, he would sit on the settee and watch Jamie and me getting ready for school. He would say, 'Come on, Kelly, hurry up! Mrs Armitage will be waiting for you.' (Mrs Armitage was by far my favourite teacher, so nice in fact that it was almost like having my mum as a teacher.) One morning, a friend of my dad's popped round (he came every week) as he owed Dad money. That particular day, all of a sudden this man was flat out under the ironing board – my dad had floored him with a right hook. Then, to our surprise, he picked this chap up off the floor, sat him up in an armchair and asked Mum to put the kettle on.

'Make a nice cuppa, will you, Val?' he said.

Eventually, when this man came round from his sleep, Dad said, 'Alright, me son, don't be late again. Good boy, go on, get that nice hot cup of tea down ya!'

'Val, I think he's learned his lesson, don't you?' Dad said to Mum. 'I don't think he'll be late again.'

Again, episodes like this became the norm in our house. I said earlier that life was very different to the norm in the McLean family household, so I guess by now anyone reading this book has very quickly realised I really wasn't kidding.

I really hated school and would do anything possible to get out of going there. On one of my 'days off', Mum and I were going down the local market. Back in the day, the market was so thriving and well known, you wouldn't dream of going out of the house shopping or doing errands without being completely done up to the nines. Anything less than being totally togged up would be completely frowned upon. After a great trip out, Mum and I walked in through the street door and heard, 'About f**king time, Pinocchio is here!' Mum looked at me a little confused: who the hell was he talking about? Dad always had a name for everyone, and that little nickname thing rubbed off on us too over the years.

When we eventually got inside the house, Mum said rather tentatively, 'Hello?,' to which Dad replied, 'It's the man from the school board, he's here about Kelly having so much time off school.'

At which point, 'Pinocchio' (or whatever his name was) reached into his satchel, took out all this official-looking paperwork and immediately began to tell my parents just how serious this situation actually was. All of a sudden I noticed Dad pulling faces right behind this fella's back. I tried hard, but could do nothing else but laugh, at which point Dad slipped into his strict parent routine and pretended to tell me off – 'Kelly, please do not laugh. You naughty girl, this is serious!' However, what the school board man could not see was the big grin on Dad's face while he was supposedly scolding me. In response, Pinocchio piped up, 'Yes, Kelly, it's not funny. Your dad is completely right, I could put you in a home for this.'

Immediately all hell broke loose. Dad went crazy: 'A HOME? Have you got kids? Get this mug out of my f**king house, Val!' In less than a second my dad had gone from a Mr Nice Guy character to a raving lunatic. Suddenly, and quite viciously, he grabbed all of the paperwork and tossed it in the air like confetti. The school board man was out of our door like a banshee, his feet did not even touch the ground.

Strangely enough, we never heard from Pinocchio again. What with this and that going on, Mum took Jamie and me out of that school. She wasn't at all happy with the place. As I'm sure you can imagine, this was not to be a peaceful exit. However, it was not my dad's temper this time, but Mum's. My brother Jamie and I could not believe our eyes when we saw our quiet, reserved Mum knock the headmistress spark out on the floor. Mum was the epitome of quiet and reserved – well, at least up to this point, the point where her kids were under attack and had been upset. In that situation, she could be almost as fiery as our dad.

Well, anyway, after Mum's little tête-à-tête with the headmistress, we quickly started to make our way off the school premises, but as we neared the school gate, we spotted a police car pulling up.

'Whatever you do, don't look back, kids. Just walk normally, as if nothing has happened!' Mum whispered from the side of her mouth.

So there we were, two little snotty-nosed ginger kids, hanging off our mum's arm, with the biggest of grins slapped across our Chevy Chases (faces) you've ever seen.

The ironic thing is having hated school, I now work in one and I absolutely love it. The principal of the academy and I have a fantastic friendship, and he has a great deal of respect for me to boot; also, our group of staff all get on like a house on fire. My girls never miss a day at school either. There's no swinging the lead in our house to get a day off school, not with this McLean!

3

LATE EIGHTIES, EARLY NINETIES

Growing up in the seventies and eighties, as I did, was so very different for us McLeans. Unlike the kids of today, we could play out and roam around the area where we lived without a care in the world – well, almost! Yes, there were still some wrong 'uns around, that goes without saying, but maybe they were more afraid of us council estate kids than we were of them. I would hang around with a group of girls, usually about seven or eight of us. Mostly, we really were a good bunch, mischievous but funny, just kids having a laugh. We never upset anyone, we just played good old-fashioned games like Run Outs, Tin Tan Tommy and Knock Down Ginger. The whole bunch of us got on really well.

Early one evening, the group of us, including my dear friend Karen Latimer, were walking down Old Ford Road past a bus stop on our way to the shop where we were going to buy some sweets. Walking towards us was a couple, a man and a woman with ashen skin and drawn faces. Basically, they looked like a pair of scumbags. It soon became apparent to us kids that they were, in fact, drug addicts. As this couple neared us, they obviously must have noticed me, and shouted over, 'Hello, beautiful!' With that, I looked round at my friend, who came from a well-known family from around the East End: 'Vicky, are they talking to you?' I said. 'No, Kel, I think they aimed that at you,' she replied.

We carried on walking, not giving it a second's thought, when all of a sudden I was being jumped from behind. As I had my hands in my pockets, they easily managed to pull my jacket right over my head. At this point I was worried they might have a knife or something, and they could quite easily have cut my face with it. All of my friends ran away apart from one: my dearest friend, Karen Latimer. 'Get off of her!' she was screaming. And with that the man punched Karen right in the face. Later, she told me that when the man hit her, all she could see was stars, but she never once left my side.

All of a sudden, through sheer aggression, I managed to wriggle free, and immediately the rage came over me; I wanted to kill this bullying bitch. As I flew for her, the man jumped in front of me and said, 'Lay one hand on her, and I'll make sure you're black and blue all over.'

I thought to myself, 'This mug doesn't know me, but I'm not going to take a chance.' 'Right, wait here while I go get my dad!' I shouted. As we were running home to my house, some other children joined us, and by the time we got to the flats there must have been about thirty kids in our wake. Not one person had told this mug of a fella who my dad was, simply because he had taken a liberty and every one of them wanted to see him get what he deserved for what he had done to me and Karen. I learned later that he had picked up an iron bar and shoved it down his trousers, waiting for my dad.

Eventually, as Karen and I were nearing the door to the flats, I was shouting, 'Mum, Mum, we've been jumped! Get Dad!'

Mum then screamed at the top of her voice, 'Len, Len, our Kelly's been jumped!'

Within a split second, she and my dad were together at the bottom of the block. Dad was fuming. Looking at Karen, he said, 'Where's the c**t that done that? What mug thinks they can touch my daughter and her pal?'

As we got out onto Old Ford Road, we immediately noticed the street was packed solid with people, loads of kids shouting stuff like, 'There's Lenny, go on, Len!' Right then, in front of everybody's eyes, my dad doubled in size and grew to the size of the Hulk. When this guy set eyes on my dad, he froze – you could see he was scared sh*tless, he seemed rooted to the spot.

Looking back, I remember thinking, 'You'll need more than an iron bar to take on my dad, you mug!' Anyway, with that, Dad gave him an almighty backhander – not a punch, just an open-handed slap. Well, it was a picture. This guy flew into the air like a rag doll and landed in a heap in the middle of the road, narrowly missing a passing number eight bus. This bully, this excuse for a man, was lying there, spark out on the road. With all of this going on, none of us noticed my mum belting seven shades of sh*t out of the woman that had been with the now-unconscious bully.

When he came to, Dad grabbed him round the throat: 'When you see my daughter and her friends, you look directly at the floor. You don't so much as make eye contact with them, you hear me, you no good lump of sh*t!' he screamed.

'I won't – honest, I won't,' the bully-boy spluttered, shaking like a leaf.

'Really,' my dad replied, 'I want to f**king kill you, but there's too many witnesses around. Now f**k off before I really hurt you!'

Barely able to walk, yet still having to do the walk of shame, the pair started to have it away on their toes. By this time a huge crowd had gathered and were laughing their heads off. Of course, this made it even more embarrassing for them. That mug will think long and hard about bullying anyone else again 'til the day he dies, especially after a clump from my dad – I mean, who wouldn't?

* * *

My best friend, Karen Latimer, is two years older than me. She was working full-time as a shop assistant in a chemist's called Parnell's along the Roman Road. Every night, she would work until seven o'clock. After the incident with the bullies, she saw them walk past the shop a couple of times. This made her nervous, so she came up to our flat and told my dad. From that day on, and for a couple of weeks after, he used to go and meet her just in case the dynamic duo returned. He would always turn up a lot earlier to pick her up. Karen loved that. He'd walk in and say to the gaffer, 'Alright, boss? Karen's finished now!' She would reply, 'But Len, it's only three o'clock, I don't finish 'til seven!' Dad would grab her playfully round her neck and march her home. No stopping to talk with friends, he just marched her all the way back to our house.

Karen's boss never once argued, he knew better than to argue with Lenny McLean. After a couple of weeks, Dad stopped meeting Karen from work and everything returned to normal – although Karen was gutted when she had to go back to her usual hours!

Karen and I were so close; from the very first day that we became friends, we instantly knew we had a unique bond, just like sisters. I think even my mum and dad could sense it, and to this day, we have the self-same loyalty for one another – no one could ever come between us.

Karen was always a big part of all our lives, and still is, for that matter. On one occasion, she buzzed up for me on the intercom.

'Len, is Kelly in?' she shouted.

'Course she is, babe,' my dad shouted back to her. 'Come on up! Kelly, Karen's here to see you!'

Karen would come up the stairs and knock on the door; Jamie would immediately open it, but as soon as she was inside the flat, he would slam the front door shut and put the bolt on to lock it. Then, with my dad's boxing gloves on, he would playfully proceed to beat the life out of Karen.

'Jamie, will you let Karen go! Karen, come on upstairs, dozy bollocks, and make Uncle Len a cup of tea!' my dad shouted out. 'Kelly's not here at the minute though, babe, she's out shopping with her mum. She'll be hours yet!'

So anyway, that was that: Karen was stuck making tea for The Guv'nor all day long. She could not leave the flat – well, not with Jamie guarding the front door with his boxing gloves on. They used to run that poor girl ragged.

My dad would always try and get Karen to make him his tea. To be honest, he only ever really liked my mum and Karen's tea. One time he asked Karen to make him some tea. 'No, Dad, she's here to see me,' I shouted.

Within a spilt second all you could hear was this giant stomping along the hallway from the front room: 'She's not your friend, Kelly, she's mine!' All of a sudden my bedroom door flew open. I was sat on my red beanbag directly opposite the bedroom door, and Karen was crouched over my record player, putting a new record on. Dad grabbed my music system, which was attached to the wall, pulled it clean off and threw it across the room, kicking everything else in his pathway – he wrecked the place.

Don't think for one moment that I was embarrassed – I can categorically state I was not. However, I was embarrassed for my dad, a grown man acting in such a way. And all because I said I didn't want Karen to make him his tea. Sometimes something as silly as a cup of tea could trigger my dad off. I was crying and tried to clean up the mess while Karen, who was obviously shocked, made him his cup of tea. You see, in my dad's head he thought smashing up my bedroom was the right action to take. He actually believed that I was totally in the wrong. That's just how my dad's head would get him at times.

As the saying goes, never judge a book by its cover, because mostly, there will be a reason behind something that a person may do. For example, my dad could never be bothered to clean his car and he just did not have the patience to watch and wait while someone else cleaned it down at the local car wash either. So, on Sunday mornings, I would hear, 'Kel, do you want to wash your old dad's car?' And I would always jump at the chance: 'Yeah, Dad, I'll do it!' I would clean it inside and out.

'She's a good girl, my Kelly. See, Val, she always helps her old dad,' he would proudly say to my mum.

Now, I never simply washed my dad's car out of the kindness of my heart. Oh no! Cleaning the outside of the car was OK, but when it came to cleaning the inside… It must have been like sitting in a mobile ashtray, but there was some cream in among all the tobacco, fag butts and ash, not to mention his secret stash of Jelly Babies (or should I say *empty packets* of Jelly Babies – my God, he must've eaten a whole colony of little jellied people!). In among all of this crap, to my delight, with a little more digging I would find tons of ten-bob bits, and not just two or three – no, no, I mean enough for a new bit of clobber. I would usually get around thirty quid's worth at a time! Just to add a little extra bonus to my half hour's graft, Dad would give me a tenner for cleaning the car. It was always a win–win for sweet little Kelly.

So I guess by now you can see there was method in my madness. I'm Lenny McLean's daughter, of course I was on a good earner! Every Sunday morning, I got about forty quid – all just for cleaning my dad's car. How he never twigged will always be a mystery, I'm telling you. I mean, he knew that I was just as tricky as he was. Well, tough luck, Lenny McLean! I had you right in the palm of my hand with that little number, now didn't I, me old son?

Jamie and I are completely different people when it comes to things like this. As soon as he got any pocket money, it would burn a hole right in his pocket and he would have to go straight down the shop to spend every last penny. He didn't care what he bought, he just had to get rid of it, lock, stock, the whole f**king lot. However, as I said, I was the complete opposite. I would save up all of my pocket money in five purses I had hidden round my bedroom. I was incredibly frugal, like a little ginger freckle-faced Scrooge. But please don't ask me why I had five purses, because I haven't a clue. Probably another area in which I was like my dad: if I saw something I liked, I couldn't just buy one – oh no, I had to buy the lot of them!

Dad was also very sensible with his money. He would pay most of the bills as soon as they came through the letter box. He would have to sort a bill straight away, otherwise it would have driven him completely insane with the knowledge that it remained unpaid. Nevertheless, he was no saint when it came to paying certain bills, like the TV licence. This was definitely one that he would begrudge paying and would try his hardest to dodge. He hated paying it. You see, Dad's way of thinking was that because we lived in a block of flats, the TV licence people would never be able to tell which flats in that certain block had TVs and which ones did not. Also, we had an intercom system at the main entrance to the block, which meant that no one could enter without being buzzed in first. Well, that was the theory my dad had conjured up in his head anyway.

LATE EIGHTIES, EARLY NINETIES

One day I was out playing on the landing with some of my friends when three people came out of the lift, looking very official – they even had official-looking folders under their arms. They knocked on the first flat nearest the lift, my mate's flat. Back in the seventies and eighties, no one would open their door without checking first, just in case it was the Old Bill or someone else in authority. But you could always tell if it was the police at your door because for some reason they had a certain knock which was different to everyone else's. Back then, everyone would look through their spyholes first, as in those days almost everyone was into a bit of villainy in some way in the East End of London – that was just how it was. Anyway, my mate must have thought it was OK because she opened up the door. Being the nosey kid that I was, I immediately started ear-wigging.

'TV licence man!' one of them hollered.

It was too late for her: she was caught. Then again, there was no way she could have got away with it, with the television blaring full belt. I bet you could have heard their TV from three blocks away! Anyway, I ran as fast as I could up the stairs into our front room and told my mum and dad that our neighbour had just been caught red-handed by the TV licensing man. Well, that was that: the television in our flat went off immediately. We waited and a few minutes later, it was bang, bang, bang on the front door. My mum got up to go downstairs to answer it. 'No, Val,' Dad shouted. 'Sit your arse down, I'll deal with this. Kelly, give me Mummy's book and her reading glasses, I need to borrow them for a minute.'

On his way downstairs to answer the front door, he slipped on Mum's reading glasses. Now here we have a man who looks like a lunatic – all twenty stone of him – with a pair of ladies' reading glasses stretched across his face. He could just about get them on without breaking them; they were miles too small for his big head. The lenses made him look as though he was cross-eyed. He had my mum's romantic novel in his hand – Mills & Boon, I'm guessing. Not the sort of book you'd expect a frightening-looking geezer like him to be reading. With that, he opened the door.

'TV licence man!' a voice exclaimed.

Mum, Jamie and I were up the top of the stairs, waiting silently like three naughty schoolchildren for Dad's next move. The next voice we heard was that of a very well-to-do man. It was Dad, still wearing Mum's glasses, her romantic novel in his hand. In a gruff yet posh voice he said, 'Oh no, my good man, we do not have a television in this house, we are all book readers!'

The TV licence man looked at the book that Dad was holding in his massive mitt and said, 'Oh, so you're an old romantic then?' A little confused, Dad looked at the book and this time forgetting his posh accent, in his gruff voice he replied, 'Yeah, mate, I'm an old romantic!'

With that, the man turned on his heels and went on his way. Dad closed the door, turned round to see us lot on the stairs and said, 'Eh, I'm an old romantic, I am.' He then coughed and farted, threw the book over his shoulder and shouted out, 'Val, put ITV on and make me a nice cup of tea! *Minder*'s on in ten minutes.'

Dad also tried his luck fiddling the electric too. He would slide a strip of photo negatives into the meter by slightly wedging open a little gap, just wide enough for the strip to go through. The negatives would rest on a wheel, which in turn would greatly slow its rotations down, lowering the amount of electricity we used. Knowing roughly the time that the man would be coming around to read the meter, he could then pull the negative strip out a couple of weeks beforehand, just to make sure the electric bill wouldn't be too low – well, not so low that it would raise suspicion anyway.

One time when the negative strip was in place in the meter, Dad got his dates mixed up and forgot to pull out the negative before the man came to take the reading. Mum said that the man had such a puzzled look on his face when he was reading the meter. When he left, she took a look inside the meter cupboard and noticed it straight away: Dad had forgotten to take the negative strip out from the meter altogether. When he eventually arrived home that evening, Mum said, 'That was handy, Len – the electric bill is only one pound.' To which he replied, 'Oh f**k, I forgot to pull the negative out! Bollocks! What did you say to him, Val?'

'I didn't know what to say, Len – I was put right on the spot. I just said that we had been away on holiday.' To which the electric man had replied while shaking his head in disbelief, 'What, have you been away the whole entire summer then, Mrs McLean?'

Dad just laughed, and Mum said, 'You won't be laughing tomorrow, Len – they're coming round to change the meter.'

Well, his face dropped a foot, and Mum strolled off down the hallway, laughing.

You see, trying to find an angle to save a few quid would have been instilled in my dad from his childhood days. He never had much of an education and was never at the top of the class, but what he did have, growing up in the East End, was the ability to sniff out a way to earn a quick tanner. He was educated at the school of life. As a young man he was always making deals, ducking and diving – he never held down a nine-to-five for very long because he simply could not take orders off people. Again, this stemmed back to the way that he'd been treated by his stepfather. Also, there was his split-second short temper, as I'm sure you can well imagine. A very bad combination when it came to Dad being in any kind of legitimate employment; it was his way or the highway. As my dad got a bit older and wiser, and with the added responsibility of being married and having to provide for Mum, Jamie and me, he became immediately aware of the need to get a steady and stable income coming into the house.

A friend of his was doing very well for himself – he had his own car showroom, among other things. Dad would go round and sit in his friend's office. He would sit there thinking to himself, 'One day, Len, you'll have a business and an office like this.' He would sit behind that desk with a cup of tea for hours, plotting and scheming how he was going to make his fortune; he would pick his mate's brains trying to find a move, any way possible to start up some sort of business.

His mate said to him one day that there was a newsagent's on the corner of the road that was up for sale. Well, that was it. Like a bull in a china shop, and without even discussing it with my mum or giving it too much thought at all, he had spoken to the owner and done the deal: bosh, sorted! All my dad could see through his rose-tinted glasses was a lot of pound notes coming in. He would have been picturing himself like the lord of the manor, sitting behind the desk.

So, that was the next thing: my parents were now the proud owners of a newsagent's. The shop was only small – in fact, so small that it was a squeeze to get two people behind the shop counter at once. Mum and Dad did not change anything to do with the shop; they even kept the previous owner's employee on. I guess they felt sort of obliged, as she was an elderly lady. When the shop was quiet, I would sit with her and she would teach me how to knit – I grew quite fond of her and our little chats. Despite the shop only being small, it was in a very good location, so there was plenty of passing trade. It ticked along nicely and took quite a lot of money; it was a very successful little business.

My dad saw himself as something of an executive – an entrepreneur, shall we say? – and with his newfound retailing skills, he thought it a good idea to sell up and buy a bigger newsagent's. Mum was dead against the idea: her view was that the newsagent's was doing really well, they were taking good money, the members of staff were reliable and trustworthy, they had no stress or strain, so why spoil a good thing? They could have had a nice easy life, the pair of them.

But no, once again, Dad knew best and decided it was time to move on to bigger and better things. It did not matter one jot what my mum said, Dad did as he had always done when he was a younger man and refused to listen to any advice. As far as he was concerned, it was a done deal and he was going to do it his way.

There was no problem selling the newsagent's – as soon as people took a look at the books, they could see it was making a very good living. Meanwhile Dad had his sights set on this shop in Shaftesbury Court in Hoxton. It was twice as big as our last shop. So, Mum and Dad went to see the owner and had a look at the books. The shop, according to the books, was a little goldmine – so much of a goldmine in fact that Dad was shocked that the current owner wanted to sell. Not wanting to miss such a great opportunity, he did the deal with the owner immediately without questioning why he wanted to sell such a successful business. Dad could not wait to start making all of this money that the shop was taking.

So that was it, off to Shaftesbury Court we went. Mum and Dad were moving on to bigger things and hopefully on to making their fortune. Mum was surprised that the books for the shop were in fact correct, and that the shop was doing very well indeed – money from the new business was rolling in. Maybe my dad did make the right call, this could be the cream they were looking for.

As the shop was busy, my mum asked her friend Lorraine to work with her. The two of them made a good team: one behind the counter and the other replenishing stock, etc. But most important was that they had a good rapport with the customers. Dad floated about, going to the wholesaler's, getting stock for the shop, but not really working behind the counter. There was this young girl who often came into the shop – she was in her early twenties and Dad could see that she was struggling for money. He knew this because she would pay for her fags with a handful of coppers every time. My dad had a very soft side to him, especially with the underdog, and this girl seemed to be just that. So, once again and without consulting with anybody, Dad decided to do what he thought was right and he gave this girl Tracy a job. Anyway, Mum wasn't too sure; she felt that even though Tracy was down on her luck, it just wasn't necessary to employ another pair of hands. Dad said to Mum, 'Val, don't worry. We can get her to come in at six in the morning and bring in the paper delivery.' So anyway, that was that. For the next few weeks, Tracy would arrive at six in the morning and take in the newspapers. It all seemed to be rolling along smoothly, although this didn't last too long. One day, Mum approached my dad about Tracy and said, 'Len, I think the girl's thieving off of us.' Dad said, 'For God's sake, Val, don't say anything in case she leaves! I mean, who's gonna get in at f**king six every morning and bring in the papers?' But Mum wasn't going to let Tracy thieve from us, so the very next day Tracy was gone – my mum had given her the elbow.

That was fine, but now they had a massive problem: who was going to open up the newsagent's at SIX IN THE F**KING MORNING?! They came up with this plan to share out the opening up. Mum made up a work rota and pinned it to the wall in the stockroom. Everyone would have a turn in opening up, even my dad.

It was important to open the shop at six as the papers were delivered at that time and they couldn't be left out in the elements of our Great British weather for too long, could they? The rota was working well – my mum and Lorraine opened the shop on time every day. There was also some money to be made, as people passing on their way to work would get their papers and fags for the day in one fell swoop.

But then it was Dad's turn – 'Right, here we go,' I thought. So this man, a regular to the shop, came in every day at around eight o'clock to buy his newspaper and today was no different. Anyway, as he was about to pay for his fags etc, he looked down at the pile of newspapers on the shop floor, and would you believe it, those papers were wringing wet. With that, he promptly looked up at my dad and said, 'Erm, Len, has it been raining this morning?' With a strange puzzled look on his face, Dad said, 'No, it's a beautiful morning out there, why do you ask?'

'Oh, nothing, Len. It's just I'm wondering why my newspaper is soaking wet?' the old fella replied.

With a sarcastic quick-fire reply, Dad said, 'Well, what do you expect, mate? The papers get delivered at six and I didn't arrive here until seven thirty, so the dogs must have p*ssed all over them, mustn't they?'

Well, as you can guess, along with the old boy, we lost many more customers over the next few months. To be quite honest, my dad's attitude towards them was terrible. In the end they were frightened to come into the shop because he had such a short temper, and as his character from *Lock, Stock*, 'Barry the Baptist', would put it, 'He was a f**king liability!' The customers hated it when my dad was working in the shop, he was a nightmare. Mum later told me stories that were not great for business, but they did make me laugh. Here is a short one for you...

There was this lady that went in one day for some sanitary towels, or STs as they called them back then.

Dad went to the shelf where they kept the cigarettes and was mumbling away to himself as he was going through them, 'Benson & Hedges, Marlborough, Rothmans, Silk Cut...' With that, the lady said, 'No! STs please, Lenny.' My dad returned to the cigarette shelf: 'What are STs? I've never f**king heard of them, love. You'll have to give me a bit more help here, sweetheart.' So, she bent forward and whispered quietly and delicately in his ear: 'Not cigarettes, Lenny, I mean sanitary towels!' At which point Dad went absolutely mad and screamed, 'F**k off, what are you asking me for those for, now f**k off out of my shop.' Suffice to say, the lady never ventured back into Mum and Dad's shop ever again.

Also, there was this man who accused my dad of short changing him by one penny. My dad lost his temper with him, he picked the till up (unlike the tills of today that are made of plastic, the till we had was made of metal and it weighed a ton), and slung it straight at this man. Luckily the man just managed to duck out of the way of the flying till; it smashed against the wall of the shop, money scattered all over the floor, and the fear was written all over the man's face. I think he must have feared for his life; he had it away on his toes, straight out of the door, and off down the road.

Instead of using the money from the newsagent's to go to the wholesaler's to replace stock, Dad thought that it would be a better idea to use the money to buy knocked-off gear. So, instead of the stock room being full of crisps and cans of coke, he would store all of his knocked-off gear in there. He would have boxes of trainers, Kappa tracksuits, and my favourite was the Ferrari foldaway sunglasses. The arms of the glasses would fold up so that the sunglasses could be stored in a round, foldaway zip-up case. Meanwhile the shelves were getting emptier and emptier as he just couldn't be bothered to go to the wholesaler's, and for that reason, the customers were coming into the shop less and less.

Not surprisingly, the shop was a short-lived chapter in my mum and dad's lives. Mum would tell him, 'Len, you can't speak to the customers like that.' – 'F**k 'em, Val!' he would say. No one would come in when Dad was working in there, and who could blame them? Anyway, after a few months, the shop closed. My mum and dad actually went bankrupt. Mum always said to me that it was a bad move from the beginning, selling the first shop to get an even bigger one, and how right she was. Nevertheless, just because the newsagent's went bankrupt, this did not mean that it was the end of Dad's career in the knock-off gear arena – oh no, not for a minute!

4

IN IT FOR A NICKER

Like I've mentioned earlier, my dad loved a bargain. Well, let's face it, who doesn't? This one time Mum and I were on the balcony when Dad pulled up outside. He jumped out of the car with two big black bags in his hands, smiling like a Cheshire cat. As he started walking from his car towards the entrance to our flats, the look on my mum's face was a picture: 'What the hell has he got on his feet?' Well, as Dad came into the flat and started coming up the stairs, he shouted out, 'Val, Val! I've got a right bargain here. We'll earn a fortune out of these!' Mum turned round to me and said, 'Oh, for f**k's sake, what lorry-load of sh*t has he bought now?' Dad went on, 'Look, Val, look what I've got!' You could tell from his voice how excited he was. He then said, 'Look, Val, Pony trainers – they're the absolute bollocks,' and Mum said, 'Pony, yes, I'll say, Len. I can see they're f**king pony! I mean, your feet came in the room ten minutes before you did, they look like a couple of boats!'

Mum and I couldn't hold it in any longer and the two of us burst out laughing. In fact, we were both laughing for weeks after. My dad never saw the funny side of it; he thought my mum was jealous of his new Pony trainers, he thought he looked the absolute bollocks in them. Actually, he thought they looked that good, he kept five pairs for himself – five pairs of f**king sh*t, in five different colours!

Anyway, the craze for buying ridiculous so-called bargains didn't stop there, oh no! He arrived home one day in these disgusting sunglasses, thinking he was the bee's knees. We all told him he didn't look cool, but again, would he listen? 'They're Grantleys,' he said. He actually meant Foster Grant, which were the fashion at the time, but these were definitely not Foster Grant! He thought we were all jealous of him then too! Only trouble was, he had bought a whole job f**king lot of them, pleased as punch that they were only £4.99 a pop.

The next day, Mum and Dad were going out for something to eat. Dad was done up to the nines, staring at himself in the mirror in a pair of these awful new sunglasses. Mum stood waiting, looking extremely embarrassed, and they hadn't even ventured out of the house yet.

My dad loved his Chinese food. Mum and Dad would regularly go to a local restaurant called The Lotus, which was a converted river barge. The place had been built on two levels: there was a small bar and some tables on the lower deck and more tables on the upper deck. The Lotus restaurant is still moored in the same place today, in the docks near to Canary Wharf.

So there he was, my dad in his new 'Foster Grant' sunglasses, with my mum in the car, driving to The Lotus. She was finding it hard to contain her laughter every time she looked at him. Suddenly, he swerved the car; Mum was rocking back and forth. 'That was lucky, Val,' said Dad, to which Mum replied, 'What was that, Len, what happened?' 'Didn't you see that big dip in the road, babe?' 'What dip, Len? There was nothing in the road,' she replied. With that, my dad swerved the car again – 'Sorry, Val, but there are so many dips in the road!'

'PULL OVER AND TAKE OFF THOSE STUPID F**KING SUNGLASSES!' Mum yelled.

With that, she put the sunglasses on, turned to Dad and said quite abruptly, 'Len, it's those sunglasses that are making the road look all uneven. They're a complete hazard and a poxy load of junk!' At that moment Dad realised he'd been a bit of an idiot, and while laughing away to himself, he tossed the glasses onto the back seat, never to wear them again. But no way was he going to waste the money he had weighed out on the rest of them – he still managed to sell them on to some poor bastard as a job lot. So, if you cast your mind back to the eighties, and you too thought you were driving your car through a load of dips in the road, think hard, son: did you also have a pair of my dad's poxy two-bit 'Foster Grant' glasses on? Well, hard luck, no refunds to be had here – Dad's clobber only carried a twenty-four-hour return to base warranty. Even then, I wouldn't fancy your chances, would you?

Eventually, Dad thought he would go down a different route to earn money. He didn't see the point in running around trying to get rid of knock-off gear as it was more hassle than it was worth. He decided instead to lend money to people who for one reason or another were unable to go to the bank and ask for a loan. It was a great little number for him: he could just sit at home drinking Mum's tea and let the people come to him with the money, no chasing about anymore. This, my friends, was right up The Guv'nor's street.

There was one problem for those people who

borrowed money from my dad, though, and that of course was the rate of interest that he had set: it was huge! Most of his customers could only just afford to pay back the interest, let alone pay anything off the actual debt. One man came to our house and told my dad, 'Len, I've got five different jobs, and I'm just about covering the interest, while all of the time I'm walking about like a zombie.'

'Well, I'm sorry for you, mate, but you borrowed the money, fair and square. You knew what the deal was well before you borrowed it!' said Dad.

'But Len, I can't keep my eyes open, I'm falling asleep on the job. Do you know anyone who can get me some speed to help me stay awake?' the fella replied.

My dad hated drugs with a passion, but Dad being Dad, he said, 'Yeah, alright, son, come back in an hour.'

With that, he shouted for me, gave me a tenner and said, 'Right, Kelly, go and buy the strongest sleeping tablets they sell in the chemist's,' and off I went. When I got back, he crushed up all of the sleeping tablets and put them in a little bag. He was like a kid waiting for Christmas, sat waiting for this guy to come back. When he did come back, he couldn't thank my dad enough. He asked him how much it was and Dad's reply was, 'It's on me, son. You'll be awake for days now, boy!' So off the guy went.

Dad laughed so much. Three days later, the guy came round our house to speak to my dad, telling him that the stuff was sh*t: 'I went straight to the first job, Len, and when I finished that one, I went home for my tea, took the stuff you gave me and fell straight to sleep. I totally missed going to the other four jobs. I'm in sh*t street now, what am I going to do? The firms don't want me back at all now.'

Being all heart, my dad said, 'You'll be alright, son. You were obviously so shattered that you fell asleep. Now give yourself a week off and get plenty of rest, then go out and find another job. But don't worry about the interest, we can add that on to the following week.'

With that, the man left. Well, you can imagine the state of mind this poor guy was in, he was stressed to the max. Meanwhile my dad was p*ssing himself laughing; he thought it was so funny. Mum wasn't too pleased; she came into the room livid: 'It isn't funny, you know, Len. How the hell is he going to pay you back now he's lost his jobs?'

Dad said, 'I told him not to worry, Val. I said to him, "Look, you'll get another couple of jobs soon, and I'll just add the interest on to the end."'

'But Len, it was your fault he lost those jobs when you gave him those sleeping tablets. Anyone else would have swallowed the interest, but not you, you're going to add it on to the end!' she replied.

Dad was laughing away to himself as Mum left the room. He was like that, was Dad – he loved acting the fool and playing pranks on people. Whatever the circumstance, he just loved to muck around. Sometimes his practical jokes were a bit much and occasionally they would backfire on him. You see, there was so much more to my dad than just the hard case. He loved playing around and joking with the family. We often played hide and seek, and Dad was always like a big kid, he just never grew up. He would clench his fists and say, 'Don't you dare tell anyone about this outside of the house. I'm the tough guy, and I don't play silly games!' Of course we would just laugh along with him. To be honest, I think I miss that side of my dad the most.

5

FROM CLACTON TO ELTHAM TO FIGHT A MAD GYPSY

Dad was a proper family man. Most Sundays throughout the summer, we would take trips out to Clacton-on-Sea. My mum would get up early and make a massive picnic. It would always be the same: boiled eggs, ham and cucumber sandwiches, tinned salmon with tomatoes… proper good old East End grub.

She would also make my dad a massive fry-up before we left. It's a bit different today, but back then both my parents smoked like troopers, and during our journeys in the car, I can remember quite clearly both mine and my brother Jamie's eyes streaming as we sat in the back. The car would be filled with smoke for the whole of the journey to Clacton-on-Sea. Obviously, Mum and Dad never really noticed, otherwise I'm sure they might have opened the windows or something.

My dad would always try and park the car in the same parking space opposite the beach, and even though I was only a kid, I could quickly see how his face and his whole persona would change as we drove further and further away from London. He would be a hundred-mile-an-hour lunatic during the drive through the rat race of the East End, then all of a sudden he would transform into this calm and relaxed sort of fella as we were nearing Clacton-on-Sea.

No sooner had he parked the car than he would turn to my mum: 'I'm starving, Val! Is it picnic time yet?' he would say. Mum would start laughing: 'It's only ten thirty, Len! You had a massive fry-up only an hour ago. Give it an hour or so and it will be lunchtime.' So off we would go to the beach. Jamie and I would be playing in the sand and running in and out of the sea; my mum and dad would be smoking and sunbathing. The whole time Dad would have one eye on his watch, thinking to himself, 'How long before lunchtime?' We would spend the whole day down at the beach. Being ginger, my mum would keep us well covered up, but you could guarantee that every single time my dad left Clacton-on-Sea, he would be burnt to a cinder.

We would have a fantastic family day out, and then

take a leisurely drive back home to the East End. Then it was simply a case of waiting patiently until the following Sunday, when we would once again head back to Clacton-on-Sea for yet another family day out. We would never stay too late because my dad would always have things to do, so we would have to head back to London early in the evening. You see, at that time, he was running the doors for quite a number of pubs, clubs and other businesses up and down the West End.

Dad never stood on the door vetting the people going into the clubs. His role was simply to walk through the clubs at various times of the night and have a mooch around. His presence alone was enough to let people know that Lenny McLean was connected to it and if you were going to take a liberty, you would have to go through him first. My dad was a man mountain, and at that time twenty-one stone of pure bulk and muscle. (As a fighter, his weight fluctuated massively depending on the training he was doing at the time. He went from fifteen, to seventeen, to nineteen, to twenty-one stone during his life. When training for a fight he would lose weight; if he wasn't, the cream cakes would add a few pounds and his weight would go up and down like Tower Bridge!) He had hands like dustbin lids and a terrifying voice that more than matched his frame. Believe it or not, I have seen him with my own eyes double in size like the Hulk when he's gone on the turn (lost his temper). I mean, who in their right mind would want to go up against that?

To keep in shape, my dad would use a gym over in Eltham, south-east London, called Shapes. A well-known body building gym, it was owned by a man called Reg Parker. Being from a similar world, Reg and my dad obviously knew of one another. Reg was also an unlicensed boxing promoter. Due to my dad's historical fighting credentials, he approached him about making a boxing comeback. Dad was still in very good shape and Reg knew that his reputation could still pull a good crowd in and earn them all a good few quid. Despite my dad not having had an unlicensed boxing match for around seven years, he was still up for anything. Reg asked many people in the boxing game about matching someone up to fight him, but no fighter among them was prepared to step into the ring with Lenny McLean.

At this time, Dad would often visit his pal Kenny McCarthy ('Kenny Mac' to those who knew him). Kenny used to own a second-hand car showroom. He was the East End's answer to Arthur Daley from *Minder*, and like Arthur, Kenny also had a right-hand man – a minder, to be exact – and this man's name was

Brian Bradshaw. So, Dad and Kenny were having a cup of tea in Kenny's office, seeing if there might be a chance of getting a little earner going. They were trying to come up with different names of men he could fight, and with that, Brian walked into the office. To say the least, he was quite a big lump of a man.

All of a sudden, Kenny goes, 'Right, I've got it, Len! Let's get Brian to fight you.'

Dad jumps up, all excited: 'Blindin' idea, Ken! How about we call him Brian "The Mad Gypsy" Bradshaw?' he hollered. 'Eh, what do you reckon, Kenny? That'll make him fit the bill a bit better, eh?'

At which point Kenny became a little downbeat: 'The only thing is, Len, Brian's not even a proper f**king boxer,' he said.

'Oh, don't worry about all that bollocks, Kenny, I'll just go easy on him!' Dad replied.

But there was more. Kenny goes, 'Oh, and just for the record, Brian ain't even a gypsy either.'

'Oh, f**k all of that as well!' said Dad. 'Listen, Ken, it will all add to the show. You'll see, son.' And with that he turns to Brian: 'Right, Brian me old son, you'd better get in training cos you're fighting me in a couple of weeks' time, boy!'

I can only imagine Brian's face at the thought. Oh well, Dad had said it, so I guess it was on...

Now, over the years there have been many stories floating around about this fight, but let me tell you THE TRUTH. As I said, Brian was not really a boxer, he just worked as a minder for Kenny Mac. Nevertheless, the fight was set up and a buzz was circling. Mostly, this fight was supposed to promote my dad's comeback into the unlicensed fight game. No one was going to get hurt, Dad was just going to put on a bit of a show for the crowd and nick us a few quid. Well, at least that was the plan. However, that was not to be and it all went horribly wrong.

Dad and 'The Mad Gypsy' (Brian) were standing in the middle of the ring with Roy York, the referee. Seconds before the bell for round one was struck, Brian went straight up to Dad and stuck the nut on him (headbutted him). With his head down and looking a little bit like a puzzled silverback gorilla, Dad rubbed his forehead once or twice. All of a sudden, the Lenny rage came over him, and from that moment on, the rest of the fight was for real: this moody little boxing show was about to turn nasty.

Bang! Dad knocked Brian spark out, and as he hit the canvas with an almighty thud, he proceeded to stamp on his head. Continuing the onslaught, he picked Brian up like a rag doll and repeatedly hit him in the face. By this time though, Brian was unconscious and of course he knew nothing of what was happening to him. Then all of a sudden it was mayhem in the ring; there were fellas running all over the gaff. It took five or six burly men to pull my dad off a battered and bruised Brian – to be quite honest, they were struggling like crazy to restrain him. Nick Netley was one of the restrainers and he's a huge lump on his own. All of a sudden, my dad got free. Still full of extreme anger, he had another go at Brian. Luckily, this time the men managed to calm him down and get him out of the ring.

Immediately after Dad had climbed through the ropes, a doctor stepped into the ring. This was done with some urgency because Brian was still out cold. Between the doctor and Roy York, they promptly put Brian into the recovery position before hurrying him off for treatment at Barts Hospital.

As I'm sure a great many of you will recall, the assault on the supposed 'Mad Gypsy' was deemed so violent and brutally terrifying that the footage made the ten o'clock news, and a call to ban unlicensed boxing was immediately announced. Meanwhile Brian stayed in hospital for a couple of weeks until the swelling and the bruising had gone down, and also to make sure that there was no internal bleeding or other extensive damage.

The day after the fight, my dad was in total shock

when Kenny Mac rang to inform him of the extent of the damage that his assault had done to Brian, not to mention the fact that Brian was still in hospital. Dad was mortified, but said that he really could not remember much about the fight at all. He told my mum that Brian had headbutted him, but the rest was all a blur. This explains a lot, because my dad would often black out when he went into one of his uncontrollable rages.

With Dad feeling terrible about the repercussions of the fight, he got himself suited and booted, and made his way straight up to Barts Hospital to visit Brian. When he walked onto the ward and actually saw him, he was completely gutted at what he had done and could not apologise enough, he said. Dad carried on visiting Brian throughout his stay in hospital, and the pair remained friends from that day forward. Brian never held a single grudge against my dad – that was just the old-fashioned East End way, you see. Two men would have a tear-up (a fight), and whatever the outcome, it would never be mentioned again. Sadly, Brian and of course my dad too have now passed away.

6

A STRETCH TOO FAR

In the summer of 1991 I was twenty years old. The sun was rising on a beautiful Sunday morning; it was deadly silent, very peaceful. There was no noise at all, just the sound of the birds practising their dawn chorus.

The first one up in our house, I went to the kitchen to make a nice cup of tea. While I was waiting for the kettle to boil, I stared out the window. Oh my God, I couldn't believe my eyes! The length of our street was full of police cars and meat wagons. What was going on? Was I dreaming or something?

In the blink of an eye there was an almighty bang at our front door. This was no dream. The only people who knock like that are the Old Bill, and the street was teeming with them. I knew immediately who they were there for and so I ran as fast as I could and woke up my mum and dad. I was in a terrible state: 'The street's full of them, what have you done?' I shouted. And then 'What happened?' at the top of my voice. Again, BANG, BANG, BANG on the front door. In a broken voice, Dad said, 'Don't worry, Kel, it's the other people they want to speak to, not me!' He looked over at my mum and said, 'Val, open the door and then make me a cup of tea. Tell them I was getting dressed and I'll be down in a minute.'

I don't think it had quite sunk into my mum's head, she seemed to be wandering around in a complete daze. She opened the front door and in came about twenty Old Bill. How they squeezed into the kitchen, I don't know. They were very respectful towards us. Mind you, I wouldn't have expected anything else – they knew how aggressive my dad was. Listen, they were police officers, they're not dumb – well, at least some of 'em ain't!

Mum offered them all a cup of tea. All of them declined apart from the main officer. He sat at our kitchen table, cup in hand, sipping my mum's famous tea. I bet my dad was thinking, 'Cheeky c**t, drinking Lenny McLean's tea!' I knew my mum was thinking, 'Thank f**k the other nineteen said no!' – she didn't have enough cups anyway.

The atmosphere was tense in the house; the police didn't know how it was going to go. I'm sure they were briefed about how temperamental my dad was, how he could go on the turn in a split second. Once again, it fell silent. All of a sudden there was an almighty boom, boom, boom, like the sound of a giant coming down the stairs: Dad entered the room.

Before they could say anything, he said, 'I'm going to have this cup of tea and then I'll come with you.' He sat at the table with the main copper and his tea. I couldn't believe how calm he was; he just sat there while everyone else stood and stared at him. The conversation between my dad and the main copper was also calm and civil. If I'm honest, this shocked me a little. I remember the officer apologising about the way they came to arrest my dad. I could see where they were coming from – Dad's reputation for violence was well documented. His short temper meant that the police could not afford to take any risks; they had to approach the situation with extreme caution.

Dad wasn't silly, he was streetwise; he knew how to approach certain situations as well. He knew when to blow his top and when to stay calm and think clearly. The police weren't silly either – they knew the best way to play my dad. They never handcuffed him. I think they knew this would only antagonise him and could set him off. My dad was cut from the same cloth as his notorious bare-knuckle fighting uncle, that being Jimmy Spinks, The Guv'nor of Hoxton in the 1940s and 1950s. Like with Jimmy, everyone knew that if you wanted to have a row with my dad, you'd better bring an army of fellas with you. Listen, they didn't refer to him as Ten Men Len for nothing, now did they? Anyway, he stayed calm and off he went to the station for questioning. My mum and I were left dazed and confused in the house.

'What do we do now?' I said.

Mum said, 'I haven't a clue, Kel. I'll phone Mick.'

Mick Theo was one of Dad's closest friends. Like most people, we know a lot of people, but we only have a handful of real close friends.

After Mum had explained to Mick what had just happened, he came round to our house and took my mum down the station. He had mentioned there was an incident at the club the night before and that my dad had given this geezer a backhander. It was probably to do with that and not to worry, he said. Not to worry? Now that would turn out to be a massive understatement of the highest order to say the least.

So, I stayed at home with my friend Karen Latimer, who came round. The two of us just sat there staring at the phone, urging it to ring. We sat and stared for hours until finally, my mum rang: 'I'll be home in thirty minutes, I'll explain everything when I get there.'

Now, the two of us switched our focus, and we were both staring at the front door with one eye on the clock, counting down the minutes, which seemed like a lifetime. Mum eventually arrived home; she sat down with Mick standing next to her. She looked straight at me and said, 'Daddy's been nicked for murder!'

With that, all of the emotion that had built up inside her came out, and she collapsed in a heap on the floor – it looked as if she was going to die. Mick picked her up off the floor and Karen promptly rang 999. I wasn't any help at all, as I too was having a panic attack after seeing my mum was having one. What a pair we were! By the time the ambulance crew arrived, Mum had come round, and thankfully I was feeling a lot better too.

The medic checked my mum over and explained that she had had a very bad panic attack; they also asked us if she had received any bad news recently. Immediately I looked at Karen and sarcastically said, 'Any bad news? You've put that mildly!' and for a split second, she and I laughed.

The rest of the day was pretty much a blur. Mum, Karen and I were as you would expect – in a state of shock, mixed with a feeling of 'What do we do now?'

Mick stayed with us and tried to reassure us that everything was going to be fine. He then made arrangements with my mum to go back to the police station in the morning, so that they could hopefully get some more information.

After a very long and sleepless night, Mick came to the house and drove Mum down to the police station to see my dad and obviously to find out what was happening. To their astonishment, overnight the police had charged Dad with murder, and they had taken him to Brixton prison in south London, where he would remain on remand until his court case was heard.

As he was now a prisoner on remand, my mum was entitled to visit my dad every day. This was something he took full advantage of. He expressed that he only wanted to see my mum, Jamie or me. Before too long, Mum had lost track of the days and weeks as every single day was the same routine: get up, shower, have breakfast and then drive to Brixton prison and go through all the rigmarole of getting in. Every single day being interrogated by my dad before driving home to try and function in some sort of normal way, single-handedly running our now shattered household.

One Sunday morning, Karen stayed at my house

– in fact, she was practically living with us by then. Anyway, as usual, my mum was already up and going through her daily routine: shower, breakfast… Well, you know the drill. Bear in mind that it was a Sunday morning, and Mum is shouting up at the top of her voice: 'Karen, come on, babe, it's seven o'clock, you're going to be late for work!'

Karen shouts back, 'It's Sunday, Val!'

Now we have a bit of a problem because my mum was a bit mutton (deaf).

'What's that, babe, you want some toilet paper?'

'No, Val, it's Sunday!' Karen hollers back.

This time Mum hears her and goes, 'Oh, f**k it, Kal! You go back to sleep then, babe.'

'Sleep, Val? I'm wide awake now, I might as well get up!'

Poor mum didn't know if she was coming or going, bless her.

Most of Mum's time was spent going up to Brixton prison to visit my dad. She would always get made up to the nines to visit him and looked very pretty. Bear in mind that my dad was Lenny McLean 'The Guvnor' so for an easy life, the screws wouldn't limit his visits to the standard one hour. Oh no, Dad's visitors could stay as long as he wanted them to. Of course, this was great news for him, but my poor mum had to listen and answer the same questions, day in, day out, for what seemed like a lifetime. This is how the conversations would go…

'Have you spoken to the solicitor?'
'What did the solicitor say?'
'Does he sound positive?'
'How long does he think I'll get, will it be twenty-five years?'

The same questions, day after f**king day! Aaaaarrrrrgggghhhhh…

In 1992 we had a beautiful summer weatherwise, and due to our good fortune, Dad would throw this line of enquiry into the mix. He'd say to Mum, 'You ain't sitting in the garden enjoying yourself while I'm stuck in here, sweating my bollocks off, are you?'

And Mum would say, 'Of course not, Len. We're all sitting indoors with all of the doors and windows shut!'

'Good girl, Val,' he'd reply, as an ear-to-ear grin would appear on his face, picturing us lot baking away indoors.

This did, however, drain the life out of my mum, and by the time she got home after another day from hell, she would just sit in the front room, all washed up and pasty-faced. She was completely shattered.

A STRETCH TOO FAR

Jamie and I were called into the front room for a family meeting. Mum said, 'I can't keep doing this, he's draining the life out of me. I'm absolutely shattered. I just can't keep doing these visits on my own!' So Jamie and I decided to share her burden and split the visits between us, going with Mum to see our relentless dad.

The plan to share the burden and take some pressure off Mum sounded good in my head, but in reality it didn't make the slightest difference. Nothing really changed because Dad was still fixated on Mum the entire time. He would always direct the same half a dozen questions at her. If I'm honest, I felt kind of invisible. It was as if I didn't exist – it was a waste of time me even being there.

One thing Mum conveniently forgot to mention when telling us about her prison visits was that in between every question, Dad would lean over to her and give her a kiss and a cuddle. Now, I'm not just talking about a peck on the cheek, oh no, this was a full-blown kiss, with tongues and everything. I could have died right there on the spot. I just wanted the ground to open up and swallow me whole. It now became clear to me the real reason why my mum was so drained after each and every visit: it wasn't just the half a dozen questions, as if that wasn't enough.

No, she then had to endure my dad's tongue full blast down the back of her throat, day in, day out!

I will just say this: Dad being in prison took its toll on me too. This pressure was too much for me to take. I stopped eating and started to suffer with anorexia, and this, along with the worry of my dad being charged with murder and having to see my mum in such a state, completely drained and worn out… well, that did not help at all.

My weight dropped dramatically. I was five foot seven inches tall and weighed seven and a half stone. No one actually noticed my weight loss, because they were all totally fixated on Dad. Any cries for help just passed them by. This made me feel totally worthless: I felt as though none of them cared about me, and for all intents and purposes, I didn't matter one bit to a single soul. My health got worse, and gradually and silently, the depression crept up to eat into me mentally too. I shut myself away from the world.

It was easy to put it all down to my dad being in prison, and thirty years ago, asking for help wasn't an option – you would just have to suffer in silence. As you read on, I will explain to you the real reason behind my illness.

From a very young child, I kept a dark secret from everyone.

7

PRISON RELEASE, YET NO RELEASE FOR US

I have recently found out something that my dad never shared with me, through the Facebook page I run dedicated to him. Mark Davies, who did a bit of bird (prison time) with my dad in Brixton, got in contact with regard to how concerned Dad was about my health. It gave me a 'proper gee', as my dad would say; it made me feel so good in myself, hearing how strongly he cared for me. I only wish that he had shared his concerns with me himself twenty-five years or so ago. I know in my heart that he loved me dearly, as I also know just how hard it was back then for men and women to express their emotions and let family and other people in on their true feelings and thoughts. For me, I just think, 'Why not try and take a deep breath, think positive and say what you need to say? You never know, the person you are opening up your heart to, like me, might have been waiting years to hear you say those words.'

In the hope that this doesn't sound bad, without my dad demanding my mum's constant attention, as he was no longer around to do this, a door eventually opened for me. I now had a chance to spend some quality time with Mum. This comforted her greatly, and thankfully, it helped me with my depression and recovery from anorexia too. Well, most of the time it did anyway!

One night, I came home after working an evening shift at my Uncle George's pub. My mum would treat us to a takeaway a couple of times every week. Her favourite was Indian. Because my dad was in prison, she could have it whenever she wanted to. He hated the smell of Indian food, and as he was mad on his Chinese food, whenever he was home we were stuck with Chinese all of the time.

I entered the room, where my mum, Jamie and Karen were getting ready to serve up the food. I sat my five foot seven, seven-and-a-half stone frame down onto the chair and Mum went, 'Here, babe, here's your plate of lettuce.' Now, if you have ever suffered with an eating disorder, you will empathise with me here when I say that my eyes and belly were saying, 'Eat three plates of the Indian takeaway,' but my head just would not allow me to do it. It's like OCD of the brain.

So, I'm sitting around this table with my plateful of sh*tty lettuce when what I really wanted was what they were all eating. I could feel myself getting more and more agitated, watching them and hearing the sound of their knives and forks going back and forth from their plates to their mouths, enjoying their food. Eventually I told my mum, 'I want what you've got!' So she immediately got up from her seat, got another plate and proceeded to give me some of her food. With that, I was crying, doing what we in the East End call throwing a 'Sarah Bernhardt' (a hissy fit, after the extremely dramatic silent-movie actress)! Well, I did a very good impression of this, stomping all around the kitchen.

Mum picked up everyone's plate to put them in the kitchen sink. She shouted out, 'I've got him in there, looking at twenty-five years, and I've got you looking like a skeleton. I honestly don't think I can take any more!' With that, she ran out of the room, crying. I followed her up to her room and reassured her that I was trying to beat this illness; I didn't want to upset her any more. I gave her a cuddle and we lay on her bed, emotionally drained, not saying another word to each other all night. We didn't need to talk anymore; we fell asleep in each other's arms, knowing we had each other.

Thankfully, my dad was found not guilty in the end, and rightly so; he was just charged with GBH (Grievous Bodily Harm) Section 18. He served about a year and a half altogether. It was, however, a travesty of justice, a witch-hunt. The pain and trauma that unfolded over the coming months caused utter devastation to our family, something I will never forget. Dad carried that burden of murder on his shoulders for a couple of years, and I believe that it did untold damage to his mental well-being and maybe even his physical health too.

Having a parent or a loved one in prison changes the whole dynamic of the family unit. Put into the mix that said person, if found guilty, could easily be looking at a sentence in the region of twenty-five years, then to many families this could obviously feel like that person has passed away. Questions like, how are they going to do all of those years in prison? How are we going to cope without them being here? These, among a million similar questions, will be racing through their heads. The smallest of thoughts gather pace until they reach a crescendo, resulting in a full-length horror movie being played out in real life, with each and every person playing their part.

You see, as I'm sure you can imagine, my dad's presence in the family home was majestic, a bit like the man himself. To have this taken from us, whether for a good or bad reason, was to leave us fractured and numb. In one way we were a whole lot luckier than other families who have lost someone to the prison system, simply because my dad had money owed to him out on the street. As I have mentioned earlier, he ran a slightly unconventional loan service. Even though he was in prison, his customers still had their outstanding debts, and there was no way on earth that he was going to let anyone off paying. I mean, my dad was The Guv'nor, for goodness' sake!

OK, so we knew all of the names of the people who owed him a bit of dough, and of course when it was due, but there was one problem: the names in the book were not your usual kind of names. They didn't just say John Smith or Paul Jones, oh no! It wasn't that easy. Dad would write them down as 'Johnny the tooth' or 'Club foot Nel' – well, you know the sort of thing. We knew that when the money was due, my dad made the people who owed him come round to the house to pay him direct. So when these people started to come round to pay us, we would be looking each one of them up and down to see the club foot or this Johnny fella's lack of teeth!

Anyway, every single one of them kept to the agreement, all paying their debts on time, week in, week out. The owner of the club my dad was minding at the time also gave Mum his weekly wages, like it was his pension, because even though Dad was inside, he still had a very big pull out on the streets. At the end of the day a debt was a debt, and you had to honour the deal. I mean, nothing had changed for my mum – she still had to pay her bills – and even though Dad wasn't there in person, he made sure that she was financially secure.

He only served around six months of his eighteen-month sentence, so it wasn't long before he was home, where he belonged. We made it very special for his return, with 'Welcome Home' banners everywhere. I bought him a sponge cake with jam and cream in the middle and made it special for him in my own little way; the top was covered with blue icing and 'Welcome Home Len' in white. Nevertheless, the days and weeks after he came home weren't so easy; we had to tiptoe around, thinking hard about what we said so we didn't upset him. Growing up around my dad, the family would be tiptoeing around him, living on our nerves, treading ever so delicately in case he would go on the turn. Looking back, I can see that moments like this, and all the tension and uncertainty that they created, could quite easily have contributed to the fraught and over-sensitive nerves that I developed in later years.

When he came home from prison, wow, the intensity went up another level! He was ten times worse; the atmosphere would change in seconds with the wrong comment, and even leaning across him to get the salt cellar from the table at dinnertime would spark him off. Within seconds the table would be turned upside down, the dinner on the floor. He would be screaming and almost foaming at the mouth with anger; he was constantly charged up and ready to explode. God forbid anybody from the outside world cross him at a time as fraught as this.

Dad was old school, and like a great deal of men with his background, he could not show an ounce of emotion, or tell us, his family, what was going on in his head. He must have been struggling so desperately, the thoughts contained within him. But the only way he knew how to deal with this was to lash out, channelling his anxiety into extreme violence and aggression. Remember, all of his life my dad had to play a role that required him to show no weakness whatsoever. I mean, he was The Guv'nor, the hardest man around, so he had to stay in tune with this character, no matter what might have been going on inside his head.

During the many months he spent in prison, he must have had a lot of time to think, and I bet he came up with some answers too. But to tell people truly what you are feeling is so difficult. The easy way out is to push them away so you don't have to deal with it. Well, that's exactly how my dad dealt with it. I would not make eye contact for long, or try and get into a conversation with him, so let's face it, in a way, I too ran away from many of those issues.

Back then I would try and stay out of the house for as long as possible to avoid him. Most of the time I would just go and spend time with my friends at their parents' houses, especially Karen's, just anywhere to get away from the angst. My brother Jamie was always out and about with his friends as well. Looking back, and using the tools that I have now finally acquired after many years of professional help, I would have played it totally differently. As father and daughter we needed to talk, to air our issues without everything turning into a screaming match. With hindsight, it's easy to know these things, but our family all desperately needed professional help, because not a single one of us truly understood the many sides to each other's personality.

Twenty-five years ago, therapy was not a word used in the East End. It was seen as a sign of weakness and it just wouldn't have entered our heads to try it. You only saw therapists in Hollywood films; they weren't for the working class. People would say, 'It is what it is,' and just get on with it. Which of course with hindsight is the most ridiculous way to approach any problem.

You see, that's exactly what my poor mum did: unlike me, she couldn't escape, so she just had to pull up her boots, drag herself up from the doldrums and get on with it. There was this huge dark cloud hanging over the house and we were all depressed because of it. None of the family or any of Dad's friends would come round to visit – he would start on anyone who came into the house. The postman put the letters through the letter box too loud, a car was making too much noise going past… anything he could find to have a dig at, he was on it like a raving lunatic. So there he was, starting on my mum again. I had always stood up to my dad, but this time I stayed in my room, terrified at the thought of what he might do to Mum and me.

To this day, I'm ashamed of myself for not coming out of my room and sticking up for Mum. The final straw was when my brother eventually retaliated, and at this point, Jamie and Dad nearly had a full-on fight in the house. Having decided that he had seen and heard enough, Jamie shaped up to our dad, and now there were two people raging at each other, two grown men my mum loved dearly, both ready to go to war with one another. With that, Mum summoned up her inner strength and shouted at my dad, telling him this time he had gone way too far, that he was killing our family: 'The kids don't want to be in the same house as you, you're making us all hate you! Not one of your friends or family wants to be around you! I'm stuck here with you, but to tell the truth, Len, I don't want to be here with you either.'

At this, Jamie ran out of the house. I suppose he must have been thinking how close he came to having a fight with his own dad, and it was too much for him to take in. But my dad finally realised that he had pushed things too far. Mum told him that he had to snap out of it: 'We're your family, Lenny. You have nobody else around you, nobody likes the person you have become. Oh yes, Len, you're feared, but more to the point, you are hated, and not just by your friends, but your family too!' This seemed to strike a chord. It must have made him finally realise the extent of the damage he was causing with his outrageous behaviour. For obvious reasons, for years nobody had ever had a go back at him.

PRISON RELEASE, YET NO RELEASE FOR US

I managed to find my brother and he, like my dad, was very upset, but I did what I could to console him. Together, we went home, finding strength in numbers. On entering the house you could feel the tension had been lifted. Like in the horror movies when the possessed demon has been vanquished, the dark cloud had gone and there was a slight ray of light shining through. My dad apologised to Jamie and also apologised for his mood swings and his behaviour generally since coming out of prison. He told us that he loved us all very much and we were his world. He put it down to the thought of being locked up in prison and losing us all to a twenty-odd-year prison sentence, the very thing he was most afraid of. However, in his mental state, the way he was treating us was ultimately leading him to that exact situation, i.e. prison, albeit on the outside, and this would have fast become a reality, had he not immediately changed his ways.

While Dad was away, he made some friends, a few of whom turned out to be hangers-on. They told him a lot of sob stories and we all knew that even though he was a hard man, he had the biggest heart. He felt sorry for them all and asked Mum to send money to them. My friend Karen was given the unenviable task of replying to them all. She was very good at making up stories and enjoyed writing. She got the job hands-down; mind you, it wasn't as if there were any other applicants!

I thought it was funny, but poor Karen, she would sit at the kitchen table and write all of his letters. He would dictate them to her and she would write them all down, word for word, and let me tell you, they weren't short! As soon as she had finished writing a pile of letters that would rival *War and Peace*, he would say, 'Lovely, babe! Give 'em to Val and she'll get them posted.' Not one of those letters ever reached the postbox – my mum slung them all in the bin. She didn't want anyone knowing where we lived because as you can imagine, some of these hangers-on were, shall we say, undesirables…

After a few weeks, Dad had not had any replies, and he was calling all of these people ungrateful slags, but for poor old Karen, it went on for weeks. In the end we had to post a couple of the letters, as Dad went to see one or two of the people. Karen would write the letter, read it to him, alter it and when he was happy with the letter, it would be posted. Every Sunday for weeks, when the replies came, she would sit, pen and paper in hand, round the table, with Dad sitting there in his underpants, rolling up a ton of tobacco and sipping away at his cup of tea while dictating his replies to her.

PRISON RELEASE, YET NO RELEASE FOR US

I think in the end Karen would have sooner done away with herself than write and read all that load of sh*t again. But that's why Dad loved her like another daughter: she was always there for him and would ultimately put up with anything.

'She has the patience of a saint, that girl,' he would say.

8

FROM THE COBBLES TO THE SILVER SCREEN

My dad was a natural mimic, he loved pulling faces and taking off people's voices. We had a home video camera and he made full use of it; he was the leading star in all of our home videos. He was always mucking about, pulling faces and telling jokes, or simply taking the right royal p*ss out of anyone and everyone. He wasn't on his own, mind – I too liked the camera on me. Dad and I would be constantly fighting over who got the most time on that video, but I must say, I was more like the supporting actor and he was definitely the main character of the show.

Looking back at the footage, it didn't matter if it was of Christmases, birthdays or holidays, 90 per cent of any given footage that was recorded was of my dad, the other 1 per cent was me inching my way in to play any supporting role. My mum was the complete polar opposite: she hated being on show and would just run away when the camera was pointed at her. This was good news for me and my dad though, because it meant more time for us on the McLean silver screen. Mind you, I will say this: Mum did make a good camerawoman.

Anyway, as soon as we had finished filming, we would all sit down in front of the television and watch what we'd just done. Dad, of course, was the one who would have to be in full control of the 'remote thingy' as he called it; he'd skim with great pace over footage of any of us, because as I'm sure you have probably guessed by now, it was all about him, The Guv'nor. He would keep rewinding his parts over and over, laughing away at himself, while taking the p*ss out of everyone else. He had this knack in front of the camera; he always had something to say and most of the time it was funny stuff.

After the video camera, the mirror was another of his best friends – he thought he looked the absolute nuts! He was so bad that he even had the front room wall decorated from floor to ceiling with mirrors.

Even when he was training for a fight, Dad would get Kenny Mac to film his sessions. Now Kenny would not just be the cameraman, he could turn his hand to anything, like interviewing my dad, asking his opinion about the upcoming fight and all that sort of stuff. I have hours of footage of my dad training and mucking about. During a sparring session, you would see Dad take his partner by the hand and start dancing with him in the ring. Most of the time this would be his cousin and dear friend Johnny Wall, 'John John', or 'Bootnose', as he was more commonly known in and around the East End. The footage of him training would be shown in various pubs in the area to generate publicity and boost ticket sales. To be honest, there weren't too many empty seats at my dad's fights anyway. The chance that he would go on the turn was always on the cards, and that was exactly what the crowd wanted.

All they wanted to see was this twenty-stone man punch, stamp and kick the life out of any opponent, and this would inevitably put bums on seats – it was simply the place to be in the unlicensed fight world for any red-blooded bloke at that time. Just for them to say in the boozer the next night, 'Oh, I was there, son. I seen Lenny McLean do this, that and the other to whoever,' that was the way it was back in the day. It just added weight to any fella's story, telling artillery for the lads down his local, plus it might even get him a cheeky drink or two into the bargain!

Certain fights even made the ten o'clock news, that's how brutal they were. So in 1995 when my dad was approached about doing some acting, you can imagine how over the moon he was. A TV producer was watching the ten o'clock news one night and he decided that Dad would fit a character in his show perfectly. The TV company managed to get in touch with my dad and they asked him to audition for the role of this character in their new show. The thought being *on the telly* and acting made Dad so happy – it was his ultimate dream and it took him away from the fighting side of things too.

After the audition, my dad arrived home in fits. What had happened was this: apparently, he went into the audition room, said what he had to say, did what he had to do, had a laugh with them all and was told to take a seat outside. When he got outside, he saw five or six other hopefuls, all waiting for their auditions. He looked at them and said, 'Sorry, guys, I've got the part,' and they all got up and left. The woman he had seen came out and said, 'Where is everyone else?' to which Dad replied, innocent as anything, 'I don't know, babe, they all just got up and left!' Obviously, he got that part as he was the only one left.

The show was called *The Knock*, a TV crime drama created by Anita Bronson. The series portrayed the activities of London's Customs and Excise officers, and Dad played Eddie Davies, a local villain who would help out the Customs team whenever needed. *The Knock* was filmed on location, mostly over south London way.

I spent a lot of time in south London and Dad knew exactly where I'd be. So he'd drive past my way and beep the horn, acting all flash in his chauffeur-driven car, grinning from ear to ear. He probably made the driver go five miles out of his way just to show off in front of me.

The Knock was a high-profile ITV show and very successful at the time, eventually running for five series from 1994 until 2000. I get a lot of comments from fans of my dad telling me how much they still enjoy watching the reruns on TV.

* * *

The circles my dad mixed in all came from different backgrounds: some were villains, others were working people and there were some from show business too. He was friends with Mike Reid, the actor probably best-known for playing Frank Butcher in *Eastenders*, although for Dad's money, Mike was more a top-drawer comedian. Anyway, Mike introduced my dad to his agent after one of his stand-up shows at the

Circus Tavern. The agent told him that he might be able to get him some work in show business.

The agent then contacted my dad to say that there was a photo shoot coming up in Southwark Park, so would he like to go over and have some photos taken to put in his portfolio? The park was only a ten-minute drive from our house so Dad accepted the invitation. On our way there, some guy came up to Dad, and with a puzzled look on his face said, 'Hello, where do I know you from?' And then he said, 'Oh, hang on, it's coming back to me now. You're from *The Knock*, aren't you?' Well, that totally made Dad's day. He shook the guy's hand and thanked him. He loved the fact that people were recognising him for his acting, not simply for his reputation and all of the fighting.

My dad also made a few adverts. One that stays in my mind is an advert that he made for Dettol disinfectant. Not for Dad's Oscar-winning performance – no, not just that! There are two reasons. The first is that they did a close-up of Dad smelling the fragrance – well, his head covered every corner of an entire 40-inch TV screen. The second reason is that every time a commercial is shown on TV, the actor is paid a fee. For this particular advert, my dad was paid £250 every time it was shown. Every evening, we would have to watch ITV, but not because of the programmes that were on that night. No, we turned on to watch the commercial breaks! At the end of Part One of *Coronation Street*, it went silent in our house, and then all of a sudden it would be, 'There you go, Val, that's £250!' Next show, it was the same drill: all silent for the ad breaks, and then again Dad would go, 'There you go, that makes it £500!' He was earning over £1,000 a day. We were all over the moon, as adverts normally run for at least a couple of weeks, so it looked like we'd cracked it.

The advert was shown on the television for a couple of days. In my head, I was already sorting out what car my dad was going to treat me to. The next day we turned on the TV, looking forward to watching the adverts to see if Dad's commercial was on. All night, nothing, the commercial was not shown once, so obviously Mum and Dad were thinking, 'That's weird, what's going on? Why is his advert not coming on the television?' After another couple of days, Dad's agent phoned. The agent explained that for one reason or another, the commercial had been taken off-air. You could tell by my dad's face that he was totally gutted – he wasn't angry, just disappointed. We were all thinking, 'What was it, what had just been said?'

As I have found out myself in my own life, you can never totally forget, or should I say, put your past 100 per cent behind you. No one can change what has happened; you cannot get that time back and alter events. But as time goes on and emotions change, thoughts change and you can look at situations in many different ways. There is always a reason behind a certain event, reasons why it happened and different views that may have triggered the process.

It turned out the Dettol commercial was taken off the television because the family of the man my dad was accused of murdering found it distressing. At this point, I feel I must add that in a court of law, Dad was ultimately found not guilty of the charge. Suffice to say, the family involved contacted the television complaints department, who then decided to stop the running of the advert – I guess it helped the family to get on with rebuilding their lives and I can appreciate how difficult it must have been for them. But as his daughter, I thought, 'What about the damage done to my dad?' It was like he was being punished all over again. He felt that he was an innocent man, but that he was looked on from the outside world as some sort of disgusting murderer. This preyed on his mind: was he always going to be judged because of his past?

So, back to the case… Dad was found guilty of GBH and served six months in prison, which was a third of his sentence. My dad felt that even though he was now a free man, in other people's eyes he was still this thug. So he tried to change as a person. At home, we were all a lot more relaxed around him, and the atmosphere was a whole lot lighter and calmer; we were happy as a family unit. Instead of him psyching himself up to have a fight or play the role of Lenny the enforcer, the minder or the debt collector, my dad was at home, running through his lines with us. We all played the other characters in the scripts, it brought us closer as a family. Now we had something in our grasp that the whole family could join in with. When you think about it, in that way we were all back on the family video camera again with yes, you've guessed it, Dad playing the f**king lead again! Oh well, let him... I mean, he was getting paid a handsome few bob for it this time, eh?

My dad was over twenty stone, and let me just say this, the weight wasn't fat, it was mostly muscle and sheer bulk. Dad was a ridiculously powerful man all of his life, and as a man and a force, in his younger days he was extremely dangerous too.

My dad certainly mellowed a lot as he got older, but no matter what he did, he would always be labelled in that all too obvious stereotypical way. Now I'm not complaining on behalf of my dad, and he himself would be the last one to do so, but let's face it, this stereotypical image carried with it the reputation that earned him a huge amount of respect, and some vast amounts of money to boot.

All of this that I have just explained was indeed 100 per cent true, until in 1996 he was offered a role in the big-budget American movie *The Fifth Element*, or so my dad thought! Now you would have thought this would have been a chance for Dad to boast about his role in some Hollywood blockbuster, but no. Even though it was a good experience for him to sample just how big-budget movies like this are filmed, he never told a single soul about it.

You see, here's the kicker: the character he played in *The Fifth Element* was a policeman from the future, although that wasn't the only problem with this film. The issue that my dad was highly embarrassed about was the outfit that he would have to wear. It left a lot to be desired, shall we say. I will spare his blushes a little and not go into too much detail. However, it made him look like the Laughing Policeman – you know, the one on every seaside pier front across the country, the copper in the glass case. Yeah, well, Dad looked like that. Sorry, Dad! Please forgive me, eh?

Anyway, Dad was on set for a couple of days filming in his policeman's role, but to his and I must admit our delight, after the film had gone through the editing stages, he was in it for only about a split second. Listen, if you blinked you would have missed this epic cameo. 'Thank f**k for that!' I can hear him say. But let's go back to the first day of filming... Well, we were all waiting at home on the edges of our seats in anticipation of Dad's return, eager for him to tell us what it was like on set. You know, who was there, what did he have to do, did he get the hump with anyone, that sort of thing. Anyway, when he finally arrived home, all he said was, 'There was this lovely young man who was very helpful to me. He never once moaned, always had a smile on his face, nothing was a problem for him at all.' To explain, on the sets of big blockbusters they have these young up-and-coming stars who are starting out in the entertainment game working on the set as runners. Basically, they are there to run around getting stuff for the more senior members of the cast and crew. Senior members, I said, now just remember that little detail.

So anyway, Dad saw this runner, or at least that's what he thought this person was. Dad was going to him, 'Here, son, can you get me some baccy from down the shop?' and 'Can you make Uncle Len a cup of tea?' So the fella's obviously seen the size of my dad and how scary he looks, and he just obliged him on every touch and turn with, 'Yeah, no problem, Lenny,' 'Course I will, Lenny,' 'Whatever you want, Lenny.'

Dad said this young man would get on with anything, no fuss – he was such a nice person to talk to and also a bit lively on his toes, getting down and back from the shop for him.

Just to let you know how alike my dad and I are: my dad would bore the life out of you, telling you what he'd been up to throughout the day, and my husband too has to endure the self-same thing, me going on about my daily antics. Anyway, for some reason Dad didn't talk a lot about his day's filming, and let's face it, now we all know why.

So, back to the story... On the second day of filming, Dad arrived at the studio and immediately made a beeline for his new best friend, the runner: he wanted him to get him a cup of tea and a bacon roll. But to his annoyance, this 'runner' fella was nowhere to be seen – he couldn't find him anywhere. So, that's Dad gutted – he'd had it all worked out, the fella's entire day planned out for him, running errands all over the shop.

As it happened, Dad sees a spark (an electrician). He sees this spark he had spoken to the day before, and Dad goes to the sparky, 'Here, boy, where's that runner from yesterday?' To which the spark replies, 'Here, Len, you do know who that "runner" was, don't you?'

'No, I ain't got a clue, boy, but I'll tell you what, he's

very quick on his feet. The tea's always f**king red hot when he goes and gets me a cup!' says Dad.

So the sparky replies, 'Len, it's Lee Evans, the comedian.'

So, Dad makes out that he knew who the spark was talking about and replies, 'Oh, is he?'

Now I know for a fact that my dad didn't have a clue who Lee Evans was. No disrespect, but it didn't make a blind bit of difference because as soon as he set eyes on him, Lee Evans got it again: 'Here, son, go and get Uncle Lenny a nice cup of tea?'

I can picture Dad now; I could always read him like a book, my dad. Anyway, Dad never spoke about those couple of days filming on *The Fifth Element* again, unlike the next major role he was handpicked for.

9

THIS GUY'S GONNA MAKE ME RITCH

With Dad's newfound fame, his profile rose and he was given a role in one of the biggest British movies of the nineties. Unfortunately, he did not live long enough to witness the accolades. This movie was of course Guy Ritchie's *Lock, Stock and Two Smoking Barrels* (1998), a film that kick-started the careers of a great number of budding British actors including Jason Statham and Jason Flemyng. My dad was cast as Barry the Baptist, a role familiar to him as an enforcer and one most of you would agree was made for him. All his life he had to play the role of the enforcer, the minder and the debt collector, only this time, instead of making lots of enemies, he gained a wealth of fans (and made a few quid into the bargain too, of course). *Lock, Stock* hugely exceeded box-office expectations and was viewed by millions of people around the world. It was also critically acclaimed and went on to be nominated for a BAFTA for Best British Film.

Unfortunately for Dad, this epic Brit flick didn't kick-start his acting career. This wasn't due to any lack of acting ability, though. Unbeknown to Dad and the rest of us, by that time he had developed lung cancer, which was to become the biggest fight of his whole life. This was an opponent he could not beat with his bare hands; this was a fight he simply could not win.

During the rehearsals for *Lock, Stock*, Dad was weighing in at around the twenty-one stone mark. I'm told the camera adds another stone onto anyone, thus making him look huge on screen. The film people felt that my dad was too big for the camera, so they asked him to lose around three stone, bringing him down to around eighteen – still a big f**ker, but a shadow of the man we all knew just months prior to this. It wasn't a problem for Dad, he just had to make a few little lifestyle changes.

One of the biggest things to go first was takeaway food; this was cut out immediately. By then Dad's love for a prawn ball or a portion of crispy duck had reached astronomic proportions. His other main problem, as a result of minding the club doors at night, was his late night snacks.

According to his great friend, another formidable enforcer, John 'The Neck' Houchin, known in London simply as 'The Neck', my dad had an overwhelming love for Coca-Cola. John said that while working, Dad went through bottle after bottle of the stuff. John told me: 'I did try to tell Len, but Len just said, "Well, I don't drink booze or take drugs, so what harm's it doing me, eh, boy?" That was Len all over.'

Going back to Dad's weight loss, I will give you an example that proves just how alike my dad and I really are. After I gave birth to my twin girls, Prudence and Ruby, my weight was about fourteen stone – my normal weight is closer to ten. I tried on a shirt that I'd been wearing before I was pregnant, and I kid you not, I couldn't even get the shirt sleeves past my arms, let alone get it on properly. My partner Scott said, 'You might as well sling that shirt in the rubbish, you're never going to be able to get it on again!' Now that's like a red rag to a bull where my dad and I are concerned. And just like when those producers said to Dad about losing the weight, I too saw it as one great challenge, and within four months of Scott saying what he'd said, that shirt was swinging off me.

Right, so back to my dad's efforts to lose the three stone… Well, it went a bit like this…

Breakfast: now instead of the usual fry-up consisting of eggs, bacon, sausages, beans, mushrooms, bread and butter – the full monty – my dad went all upmarket and had two poached eggs on two slices of brown toast, with just a sliver of butter. To be honest, I think he thought that he was posh, eating poached eggs.

Anyway, Dad arrived home after a gym session and it was quite obvious to me that he had spoken to someone up there with regard to his diet, and whoever he had spoken to must have recommended that he try a new organic cereal. So, Dad being Dad, he couldn't just buy one box and see how it went – you know, see whether he liked it or not. No, in typical Lenny McLean fashion he had to buy twenty boxes; he never changed. When I saw this new organic cereal in the cupboard, I simply could not resist it – I just had to try it.

Crunch, crunch, crunch, chew, chew, chew… it was like eating cardboard. It was disgusting, the worst cereal I have ever tasted in my life! But again, Dad being Dad, he wasn't one to be losing face over it; he would never in a million years admit how bad this organic cereal was. So every morning he would get out of bed and tuck in. Hang on, let me rephrase that:

as soon as his eyelids opened, my mum would empty all of the fruit out of a giant fruit bowl and proceed to fill it right up to the brim with this organic cereal, immediately emptying a full pint of milk over the top.

She would then say, 'There you go, Len. Your cereal's on the table!'

Obviously, she knew deep down that he hated the sight (never mind the taste) of it, but to give my dad his due, he never let on. He did not stop eating that swept-from-a-birdcage cereal until he had demolished the whole twenty boxes of it – he simply had to prove us wrong.

He finally made it through to the last box, never once mentioning that it was like eating cardboard, although that was written all over his face. One morning, my mum saw an opening for a wind-up. Holding back a smile with some difficulty, she said: 'Len, you're on your last box, you'd better order some more cereal. I mean, you must f**king love it! You've eaten all nineteen boxes.'

'No, Val, it's alright. I'm not really a lover of it, I think I'll go back to my poached eggs on toast,' he insisted.

So that was that: the daily regime went back to poached eggs and brown toast – 'Don't forget just a sliver of butter, Val!' He would then go off to the gym for a few hours before coming home for lunch. My mum would make him two ham and tomato rolls with a packet of low-fat crisps on the side of the plate, all washed down with a cup of his most favourite tea: Mum's!

Talking about crisps for a moment, Mum brought home a box of twenty-four packets of low-fat crisps, just in case Dad got a bit peckish between meals and fancied a snack. My dad would never eat anything that he would have to prepare himself – for quickness, he would cut off a bit of cheese or open a giant packet of ham and eat the whole lot. Failing that, he would just demolish a whole pack of biscuits in a few minutes flat.

Dad was like a big kid in that way. At least once a day my mum would pop down the shops – she probably didn't need anything at all; more than likely, she just went to get a bit of a relax away from the house. On her return from one of these daily shopping trips, she noticed that the rubbish bin was filled to the brim with empty crisp packets.

'Len, what's all this in the bin? There's about twenty-odd empty packets of those low-fat crisps in here, they were supposed to last you all week!'

'Val, I got a little bit peckish. Anyway, they're only low-fat ones, they won't hurt,' he said.

Mum said, 'Yes, Len, it doesn't hurt when you eat one packet, but it's a different ball game when you eat the whole bag of twenty-four! Now get up, I'll have to hoover the chair – I bet there's crumbs everywhere.'

Well, that was the end of that: low-fat crisps went the same way as the tasteless cardboard organic cereal.

After his ham and tomato rolls and who knows how many bags of crisps, Dad would go and have a sleep for a couple of hours. Please bear in mind that we didn't know at the time that he had cancer – we just thought that he was tired because of the dieting and training etc. After he had had a couple of hours' sleep, Mum would wake him with a cup of tea. He would sit down and watch a bit of telly while she made his dinner: for this meal he would have chicken or fish and chopped tomatoes, with new potatoes and a couple of slices of bread. Oh and, I must quote my dad once again, 'just a sliver of butter'. His dinner never strayed from this path; every night he would have the same food on his plate, and every night my mum would have to endure the same line of questioning.

'Val, how many calories was in that dinner?'

And every night she would make up the same answer, because Mum didn't have a clue. Nevertheless, she knew that if she didn't make up an answer, she would have to face another half a dozen questions. It was far simpler just to spin Dad the odd line.

The only problem with this was that my mum didn't have a great memory, so now and then, she would get the number of calories in his dinner completely wrong.

Sharp as a tack, Dad was straight on it: 'Val, why are there more calories in my dinner tonight than last night?'

Equally sharp, she'd say, 'If you already know, why do you constantly keep asking me?'

This is another similarity that my dad and I have: I always have to ask questions. Even though I already know the answer, I just have to ask. It must drive my Scott mad. I suppose it's just to get some sort of reassurance, probably to do with low self-esteem, and my dad was exactly the same. I'm sure that he must have felt that he was being constantly judged.

As a child, I never thought that I was good enough and I know that my dad felt the same. He was constantly belittled and physically and mentally abused by his stepfather. Day in, day out, he was shouted at and beaten, and that kind of cruelty has a lasting effect on a young boy.

My dad never beat me, but like a lot of dads back then, he never showed me much love either. It was all left to my mum to deal with: his job was done. A man doesn't sit down and ask how his kid's day at school has been; he wouldn't sit and read a book to me or run through my spellings and say how good I was at them. However, not saying anything at all was almost as bad as telling me that my reading was rubbish. You see, in my head, no praise at all was like I'd failed – it was an attack on my self-worth.

Dad would come in from the pub and the atmosphere would completely change. I'd always look for something from him, some sort of praise, but it never came: it would just be about him all of the time. I would never feel comfortable enough to express myself for fear of rejection, and the fear of maybe upsetting the already fragile atmosphere in our house. My dad's upbringing damaged him terribly, as I'm sure it would damage any child who experienced that kind of torment. As time moves on, you don't forget those dark days either. Yes, the memory becomes less severe because you cast it to the depths of your subconscious, but one small thing can trigger it all back off again. You know the phrase 'two steps forward and three steps back'? Well, there you go... that's Dad and me through and through.

The thing is, unless you get professional help, your head will be messed up like my dad's was his entire life. The mind is such a powerful tool, it can run away with you; thoughts gather pace, and a small thought gets bigger and bigger until your head is full to bursting. People deal with it in many different ways, and my dad's way was simply to lash out, scream and shout, aggression being his quick-fire release. My way was to go back to bed and shut out the world, though I have since realised that this is completely the wrong thing to do. You need to own up to the fact that there's a problem; that is the first step, and a very big step at that. After that, if not just for your own sanity, you must seek professional help, be completely true to yourself and never hold back.

Everything needs to come out; it doesn't matter how silly you feel talking about it and telling somebody all about your troubles, opening your heart up to the person that is there to help you will not help one single bit unless they have all the information they need to help release those inner demons that are holding you.

My dad never had therapy back then, it wasn't the done thing – a man doesn't talk about his problems, a man deals with his own issues alone. It wasn't until Tony Soprano from the American TV series *The Sopranos* went to visit a shrink that it became acceptable for men with similar issues to seek help.

In my own experience, the experience that I will go into in the later stages of this book, the therapy really did help. You see, it gives you the tools needed to deal with those dark days and dark thoughts. But you must be willing to make lifestyle changes; you have to keep reminding yourself all of the time. It's like an alcoholic who goes to meetings after eighteen years of being sober – he goes to those meetings to keep those thoughts fresh in his mind so that the old habits don't creep back in and let the dark days and thoughts start taking over again.

When all's said and done, you're in charge of your own mind; you have the power to train your own mind and become at one with yourself and maybe find a little sanctuary and peace. Not just peace with the world – no, even more importantly, find the peace within yourself. Ultimately, you are the one person that it can all come back on. The fight is in your hands, and your hands alone. Other people can't help you – no, at the end of the day, you are the only one that is in control. Anyway, I have moved away from the main story a little here, so where was I? Oh yes, my dad controlled his thoughts about food and managed to reach his target weight before the start of filming.

During the filming of *Lock, Stock*, my dad kept complaining of being tired all the time. He would say to my mum that he was shattered, that he felt like he had run a marathon every day. This was way out of character – he was not the sort of man who would complain about something like being tired. Mum also knew this and so she made him a doctor's appointment.

Dad went to the doctor's without any objection. Now this was a solid sign that he wasn't well, because he would never agree to go to the doctor's ever, not for love nor money. Normally, you would have to drag him there. At the appointment, the doctor referred him to the hospital for a scan; he also had some other tests done at the same time. And within a few days, the results were back in…

Bad news… There's a shadow on Dad's lung: it's cancer.

This particular cancer was a very aggressive one, of similar strength to the power of my dad in his earlier years. It moved so fast that even though the producers of *Lock, Stock* thought that bringing the premiere forward might help, it wasn't to be.

Pride also played a huge part in this, because my dad did not want people to see him in that state: a forty-nine-year-old man who looked and felt like a man in his twilight years. One thing he was adamant about though was that Mum, Jamie and I went along with our heads held high, proud indeed of yet another of Dad's fantastic achievements. My dad died in July 1998, just over a month before the premiere took place.

We all had to make sure that we put on a brave face

because Dad had said that he didn't want us moping around the house. The premiere was held in the West End, and as we arrived in a black limo and stepped out onto the red carpet, I had incredibly mixed emotions because Dad wasn't there to enjoy it with us. It was so humbling, but at the same time it made us all so proud to have the other stars approach us and say what an honour it was to have met our dad. All of those well-known people sharing with us their heartfelt sympathies. We were, as we are today, so very proud of him.

At the end of the film, the credits rolled, and finally it said 'Dedicated to Lenny McLean', and everyone applauded him. Oh, goodness me, what lumps in our throats we all had! It was so emotional, we were so proud. To this day, that same sense of pride is within me.

What a star you were, Dad! No one will ever forget...

10

THE GUV'NOR'S LAST BOUT

Mum, Jamie and I knew we had a lot to face to get Dad through the biggest fight of his life, for this was one opponent The Guv'nor just could not knock out, no matter how big, strong and fearless he was. This was set to be the rockiest of emotional roller-coaster rides.

From that day on our lives were constant trips back and forth with Dad to the hospital for tests and appointments. This was something the whole family did together – we all wanted to be there to support him. Why is it that something as tragic as cancer brings a family closer together? It is something to bear in mind how we take life for granted, how we take friends and family for granted, when what should really happen is that we should embrace every day as if it were our last. It would help with the healing process after; it would stop guilty thoughts running through your head and stop those thoughts of 'What if?' that take over the brain. We all knew it was an aggressive lung cancer, and the type that would grow very quickly. We also knew that it would take a miracle for Dad to get through it, another reason why we had to be there as a unit of strength, making sure that he did not feel alone.

Just to add insult to injury, along with this aggressive cancer, my dad then developed breathing problems; even walking the shortest of journeys was now difficult for him. He would walk a few steps before having to stop and catch his breath. Imagine how this made him feel. The hospital gave him a short course of radiotherapy – they wanted to try and open up his lungs a bit in the hope that this would help with his breathing issues too.

Very soon the gaps between hospital appointments became less and less, but for me this wasn't a good sign at all: it seemed that it was a race against time, and it looked like it was to be a very quick one-hundred-metre sprint rather than a marathon.

The next visit to the hospital was a trip that really took the wind out of our sails. Recent tests had shown that by now the cancer had spread to Dad's brain. This was all too much to take in; it was like a hurricane

– bang, bang, bang, with one bit of bad news after another. Dad also developed skin allergies and he came up in cysts. 'What the f**k is happening to my poor father? How cruel the world is, life just isn't fair,' I thought. Because the cysts were so bad, he had to stay in hospital for another couple of days; a minor operation was needed to have them removed. My dad did not have much time left in this world, and to spend it wasting away in the hospital was just never in The Guv'nor's manual.

From the minute visiting time started, my mum, Jamie and I were at the end of his bed trying to give him hope. Having said that, the hope wasn't entirely for him. I think that between us we were trying to convince ourselves that the cancer would shrink, that everything was going to be alright, and that in the end he was going to get through this and life would go back to the way it was before he got this terrible illness.

Mum asked specifically that the doctors were not to tell Dad anything without her being present. We all knew that the only news the doctors were going to give him was going to be bad, and of course there was no way that we would want him to have to hear that when he was alone. Well, to our total disgust, that formality wasn't to be followed. Because one Thursday morning, at ten past seven while we were all getting ready to visit, the phone rang. It was Dad: 'Val, I have six months to live!'

'Don't be stupid, Len! Right, I'm on my way,' she told him. She was absolutely fuming. We had been with him all of the time, so why didn't they wait as instructed, why on God's earth would they tell him when he was on his own?

Immediately we rushed to the hospital as quick as we could. We ran all the way from the car and up to the ward that my dad was on, and there he was, sitting in the chair next to his bed. He looked cool as a cucumber considering the news that he had just received. The four of us had tears in our eyes. I ran around the bed and sat on his lap and cuddled him very tightly. You could see that he was absolutely gutted – he could not face us, he did not want to make eye contact, he just wanted to hold it all together. Very quickly the tables had turned, and now Dad was the one trying to reassure us.

'Kel, it's going to be alright. I will be fine, and I'm going to beat this thing, just you wait and see!' he told me.

He then turned to my mum: 'Val, I need to go downstairs for a fag.'

As soon as my dad was out of sight, Mum stormed up to the nurse.

'Lenny's obviously got it wrong, he's just told me that he's only got six months to live!'

The nurse got in contact with the doctor, who promptly came and spoke to my mum. The doctor confirmed it, and obviously deep down, we already knew: Dad wasn't mistaken at all, he did in fact have only six months at most to live.

As you can imagine my mum was absolutely livid. She was highly emotional, deeply angry and extremely upset, with a million worries racing through her mind. Like I have said, deep down, we all knew the cancer was terminal, but we were all so angry, given the fact that Mum had stated to the doctors and staff a thousand times: 'DO NOT TELL LENNY ANY BAD NEWS WITHOUT ME PRESENT!'

I remember quite vividly Mum saying, 'How dare you? What gives you the right to tell someone that they only have six months to live without a member of their family present to support them? It's not like telling someone they have an ingrown toenail! Come on, kids, let's go downstairs and see Daddy, he needs us.'

Going down in the lift, in this confined space, we all looked at each other and the three of us sobbed uncontrollably. As the lift reached the ground floor, we tried to pull ourselves together before we went outside the hospital, where my dad was having his fag.

Dad said, 'Val, go and get the car and pull it around the back.'

'Why, Len?' she asked.

'Just do it, Val. Do as I ask and don't ask questions.'

As soon as she pulled up, Dad got in the passenger seat and my mum said, 'Len, what are you doing?'

'Just take me home, Val. I want to go home,' he replied.

'I can't, you haven't been discharged yet.'

'Well, you can! Bollocks, I ain't going back in there again! Look, I'm f**ked if I'm wasting any more time in that place, I want to go home NOW!'

What was the point? It was a waste of time trying to will him out of that car. There was no way on this earth that he was going to get out; he was adamant: he just wanted to go home. Anyway, can you blame him? I mean, the damage was done, there was nothing they could do or say that would or could make this situation any better. Therefore, what was the point of wasting the last bit of time he had on earth withering away in a hospital bed? The choice was in my dad's hands alone. Listen, it's exactly the same as him having a smoke. I mean, for f**k's sake, what harm was it going to do? Because as I say, the damage had long been done. He might just as well enjoy the rest of his life doing what he loved to do.

No sooner had we set foot indoors than the phone rang: it was the hospital. They said my dad had not gone back to the ward and asked if Mum had seen him as he'd been gone a couple of hours now.

'*Seen* him? I'm looking at him right now, he's in the chair right opposite me. Look, he's in his house with the people who love and care for him, and after the news you've just given him, can you blame the man? Listen, I have to go now as I'm needed to make my husband a cup of tea.'

Before she had a chance to hang up, the person on the other end of the line started to give her a bollocking. We could hear this doctor or whoever it was saying, 'Look, Mrs McLean, we have not discharged your husband yet, and we have a selection of tablets here with all of the required instructions with regard to the dosage he needs to take and the specific times that he is required to take them.'

Mum shot back, 'Right, OK, my son will be up within the hour to collect them.' She promptly put the phone down and left Jamie to go and get the tablets – there was no way on this earth that she was going back up that hospital.

So anyway, after all this mayhem, we came to accept the dark, horrible fact that there would not be a great deal of time left to spend with Dad before the inevitable. We planned lots of things. First on the list was his favourite outing to Clacton-on-Sea – he loved Clacton. Mum went out shopping and I sat like a baby in Dad's arms, crying.

'Dad, promise me that you'll come back and tell me there's a heaven,' I said. I looked up and there were tears streaming down his face; we just sat there cuddling.

We were arranging to go to our caravan for a few days, Mum, Dad and me. Dad asked my friend Karen to come, and at this time she was in a relationship, but to be honest, she was spending more time with us. Dad said, 'Your boyfriend won't mind, will he?' Karen's reply was, 'Len, you come first,' and after a brief pause, Dad simply grinned and said, 'Well, that's a good girl, because if he moaned, I would of kicked him in the face because you *have* to come.'

We booked a four-day break, from Friday to Monday, staying at Seawick Holiday Park, Clacton-on-Sea. When I was a child, we had owned a caravan on a caravan park opposite Seawick – it was called Hutleys Caravan Park. Dad preferred Hutleys because it was basic: there was no swimming pool or clubhouse, it was just a nice quiet caravan park with, as my dad would say, 'no idiots playing up'. Although I must admit, we did used to go across the road to Seawick and use their facilities.

To be honest, we would have rather hired a caravan at Hutleys for that particular weekend, but at the time it was an owners-only site and they didn't hire out caravans. Seawick, to our minds, was the next best thing. Let's get it straight, this weekend was just about spending some quality time together as a family unit, it wasn't really anything to do with the caravan park.

Jamie had a convertible Saab that he had borrowed from a friend for the weekend. At this particular time I was driving and Dad was sat in the passenger seat, while Karen and my mum were in the back. Now this Saab had a button that operated the electric roof – it was in the central console right behind the hand brake. Dad just could not get comfortable; he kept fidgeting in his seat, all of the time leaning across and pressing the button for the electric roof with his elbow. So as we were travelling down the A12 to Clacton-on-Sea, the electric roof was forever going ever so slightly up and down, up and down, as I'm sure you can picture. Well, Mum and Karen thought this was f**king hilarious.

'I don't know why you two are laughing and finding it all so funny at this speed. The roof will blow right off and Jamie will do his nut!' I said. I pulled over, put the roof down properly and fixed it in the open position, then continued on our journey to Clacton. Then all of a sudden we heard from the back seat, 'We're freezing, can you put the roof up?' I bet you can guess my reply – it started with 'F' and ended with the word 'off'!

To give my dad his due, he tried not to lean on the button, but in fairness to him he had been sitting in the car for a long period of time. I bet it was hard for him; he had to keep moving just to ease the pain. Leaning over the centre console was the most comfortable position.

It did take the stress off the journey; it seemed to go quick, but not quite so quick as Mum's stay at the caravan. No sooner had we arrived than she became ill with a cold. Maybe she caught it going down the motorway with the roof open, perhaps they really were freezing in the back. For my dad's sake, she went home, as his immune system was so low, he really couldn't afford to pick up any illnesses because of the radiotherapy.

Jamie borrowed another mate's car and came down from London to collect Mum to drive her home. While she waited for him, she gave me the full SP. She told me the times that Dad's medication would be due, and how to inject his insulin together with how much and exactly how often he would need it. My mum was extremely upset at the thought of leaving us – this could be the last family holiday we ever had together. I was very nervous; I felt under so much pressure to make sure my dad got the right medication and dosage – I didn't want to make him feel any worse than he already did.

So Karen and I stayed with Dad. To be honest, he slept a lot – for him the caravan was like a safe haven, a sanctuary of sorts. His cancer had brought on diabetes, so with that, he had to keep a close eye on the kind of things he ate. Also, because Mum wasn't there and it was just Karen and myself, he of course took liberties: the gloves were off, he knew we weren't going to say no to any of his requests. At the end of the day the man was dying, so what difference did it make anyway?

Dad would send Karen for red-hot fresh doughnuts and Chinese, as he would put it, though God only knows where he thought we got doughnuts from. Anyway, while Karen went to get the doughnuts and a lorry-load of Chinese, I injected my dad in his stomach. This was all new to me: even though I was twenty-seven years old, I had never injected anybody, and to tell you the truth, I was terrified of needles. It's funny how you can overcome a certain fear when a loved one is solely dependent on you, though. Instinct, love and emotion must take over – I didn't give my phobia of needles a second thought.

One thought that I did have running through my head was something my mum had said earlier: she said to make sure that all of the air bubbles were out of the syringe before I injected my dad. So, as I'm sure you can imagine, for the next twenty minutes I was tapping away at the side of the syringe, hoping all of the air bubbles were out. In desperation I phoned her for some kind of reassurance, and she said very calmly, 'Kelly, the air bubbles will be gone by now!' My poor dad was just staring at me. To be honest, I think that he was more concerned about how long Karen was taking with the doughnuts and Chinese. Finally, I injected him just before she arrived back with the food. Now I could breathe – well, at least I could until the next time I had to use my novice nursing skills.

We stayed two nights, and then all of a sudden Dad took a turn for the worse: he felt terrible. 'Oh my God, was it down to me having injected him incorrectly? Were there air bubbles still in the syringe? What about the tablets? Had I given him too many, or maybe not enough?' My head was in complete turmoil. Looking back, it was most probably down to the thirty doughnuts and the lorry-load of Chinese food he had thrown down himself over the past two days.

We needed to get Dad home, so we packed up all of our stuff as quickly as we could. All kinds of thoughts were running through my head: was he going to make it back, oh my f**king God, what if he dies now? My mum should be with him… Driving home was a blur – it felt like I was driving 1,000 miles an hour all the way home. I just wanted to get him home.

As we were slowing down to come off the motorway, Dad said, 'Oh, Kelly, be careful, look at that in the road!'

Karen then pipes up, 'Ah, Kelly, don't hit it!'

'Why? Are you two hungry then? It's a f**king McDonald's bag!' I said.

We all laughed and that lightened the mood.

It was great to pull up outside the family home on Avenue Road. Mum was a lot better and somehow I had managed to get Dad home safely. He got out of the car empty-handed and walked inside; he was constantly asking Mum how much she'd missed him. Getting out of the car empty-handed had nothing to do with his cancer, it was just Dad all over. It was us who lugged all of the bags inside, while he stood and rolled himself a fag, and as he rolled that fag, immediately I knew that he was feeling a little better. I now felt a bit more at ease, knowing that we still had a little longer with him. I also think some of it was down to the fact that he was fretting for Mum, although he would never admit such a thing. I could see the relief in Mum's face; she was glad to have him home where she was in control of looking after his every need.

The day after, Dad was in bed and Karen was reading his book, *The Guv'nor*, to him. He would often ask her to read certain parts of his book to him; he mainly got her to read the last few pages. I have not read his book, because at that particular time I could not, and to this day I still cannot, bring myself to read any part of it. Karen has told me many times in the past that the part of the book that Dad made her repeatedly read to him was indeed very sad. Although I will just say this, sad as it was, my dad got a great deal of pleasure observing people's reactions as they read about how difficult certain stages of his life had been for him.

I think that my dad was a lot like me in a great many ways. For one thing, he always thought that people never cared much for his plight, which is something that I feel with regard to my life too. A question I often ask myself is, why should people care about me? They have their own problems and issues that they have to deal with in life, so do they really need to be bogged down with mine or my dad's? Nevertheless, you see the bulk of this was really what my dad's book was all about: a collection of chapters torn from the depths of his emotions. Emotions transcribed into text for all to see in the hope of creating a sympathetic or an empathetic reaction from his readers, or as he would see them today, his supporters and loyal fans. This collection of stories, anecdotes and misdemeanours would unearth to the public just how tormented his life had truly been. Oh yes, of course some of that trauma was simply a result of his own misgivings, and listen, my dad would be the first to admit it. However, many of his issues were a result of his tortured soul. All of which lay at the door of that 'evil, bullying, no-value c**t Jim Irwin' (my dad's words, not mine). See, Dad, I said you would get your gang in somewhere, did I not? 'F**king nose ointment!' as he would always call me. Anyway, for the record, my words would be too hate-filled to print. My dad's book was the stuff of dreams to him, albeit with hindsight dreams that he would never fully come to realise. However, Dad, if you're listening, we all have realised them, and we have witnessed the many accolades, and I must say, it fills my heart with pride.

Dad's biography alone was set to pave the way for his deserved bit of cream, the cream that he had strived for his entire life. You see, people never really realised the pain and anguish that he went through in order to give my mum and my brother and me a better life – for me it's soul-destroying just to think about it. But thankfully, it wasn't all in vain. I for one have benefited hugely from all of my dad's steely determination. I also have a beautiful house in a lovely part of the country for my dad and mum's granddaughters to grow up in, which I never would have had, if not for Dad's hard work and success. But I'd like to think that I have gained a great deal of respect for life, and a humbleness with regard to what I expect from life, and this is all down to me looking back over Mum and Dad's lives and ultimately thinking about what could have been. Therefore, Dad, your book was a resounding success, and I for one am extremely proud of you for it.

In between chapters, Dad would have Karen ringing WHSmith to ask them how many copies they had sold. She must have known the number off by heart. He was constantly asking, 'How many copies today, babe? Phone up and ask them.'

Dad tormented the life out of Karen – he loved her sense of humour and the fact that he could get away with joking with her in the way that he always did. One example of the banter between them was when Karen was sitting at the end of his bed reading his book to him again and he fell asleep. This happened quite regularly, but it was like when you were a kid and your dad fell asleep watching TV, and as soon as you turned the TV over he would wake up and say, 'I'm watching that!' Anyway, as soon as Karen tried to tiptoe out of the room, he would immediately shout to her: 'Sit!'

Above: Mum and Dad on holiday at their favourite destination – Fuengirola, Spain.

Below left: Me aged 2.

Below right: My brother Jamie (left) and me in one of our primary school photos.

Above: A fun-filled McLean family Christmas – our dog, Lady, was under the table not wanting to miss out!

Below left: The four of us on holiday in Spain – don't be fooled by the jumpers, they were covering up our sunburn.

Below right: My mum and her sister Debbie (left) on holiday after Mum came out of St Clement's.

Above: Me and Dad in Cairo's bar one New Year's Eve.

Below left: In Fuengirola again in his favourite café – his idea of heaven.

Below right: This was taken at home during a low point while I was suffering from anorexia.

Above: Mum and Dad at Camden Palace, where he worked on the door.

Below: Christmas at home on Strahan Road – the hat almost fitted him…

Above: Our last get-together with family and friends at home before Dad passed away.

Below: Me with Jamie and my mum at the Bancroft Arms on my thirtieth birthday.

Above: Karen and me on my twenty-first birthday.

Below left: With my friend Rachel, showing off a copy of Dad's bestselling book *The Guv'nor*.

Below right: Me and my mum getting ready for one of our famous family parties.

Above: Me and Scott climbing the Sydney Harbour Bridge during our trip around Australia.

Below left: On holiday more recently in Fuerteventura.

Below right: With my workmate Shirley – she reminds me of my mum in every way.

Above left: Me with my twin girls, Prudence and Ruby, when they were younger.

Above right: Sisters in arms.

Below: Prudence and Ruby and their gang.

All photos © Kelly McLean

THE GUV'NOR'S LAST BOUT

The next time my dad asked Karen to read his book to him, she came up with a cunning plan. She told me, 'If Lenny falls asleep this time I might as well have a sleep at the end of the bed, because every time I so much as move, he wakes up straight away.'

'Sounds like a good idea, Karen, go for it!' I said.

So off she trundles upstairs with the book under her arm, and yes, you've guessed it, five minutes later, Dad is fast asleep. So as planned, she closed the book up and decided to have a little sleep too. The next thing that happens is not the usual exclamation from Dad going 'Sit!' – no, Karen was woken by his massive great foot right up next to her face. A little startled, she sits bolt upright and says, 'Oh, thanks, Len!'

'That's alright, Kal,' he replied. 'I thought I'd give you a little nudge as you seem to have fallen asleep.' To which Karen snaps back, 'Len, I thought someone was cutting me with a razor blade! What's going on with those toenails of yours?'

Now let me explain, it was an in-joke within our house about the state of Dad's toenails – they were hard as wrought iron! You could not cut them with your everyday, run-of-the-mill nail clippers, oh no! You would break them just as soon as you even attempted to cut one of Dad's six-inch-thick talons. That's why they would always be so long – you needed an axe, and a f**king sharp one at that, to cut those things on the ends of his feet. They were always so sharp and crooked too. As luck would have it, Dad's cousin Johnny Wall, or 'Bootnose', was the only one out of the whole lot of us who would take on the job. He had what I can only describe as a set of garden shears doing the job.

As many of you will already know, Johnny and Dad were essentially like brothers – well, let's face it, they had to be for Johnny to take that particular task on. Mum would never go anywhere near his feet – I think that if she had had her way, she would rather they'd just chopped off his feet instead. Sorry, Dad, but come on, you did have feet like that Oddbod from *Carry On Screaming*!

During the later stages of his short battle with cancer, my dad developed a condition called foot drop, which meant he would drag his foot along the ground when he was walking. To be honest, he could have done with wearing a footbrace, but Dad being the kind of man he was, as you would expect, he refused point-blank to wear one. Owing to this, he would lose his balance a lot, especially on the stairs. So whenever he went to bed, someone had to go up behind him. The staircase in Avenue Road was very steep; there wasn't even any turn in the stairs, which could potentially help break his fall. Mum used to panic because if he fell, she would never have been able to stop him from crashing down the stairs.

Whenever he walked up the stairs, my dad only ever seemed to be wearing his pants. He never wore boxer shorts, he was a pants man through and through. Even on holidays, he would wear Speedos. You can imagine a twenty-stone man in Speedos and the amount of unwanted attention this would attract! As I walked up the stairs behind him, my eyes always seemed drawn to one of his gunshot wounds – he had a chunk missing out of his bum that was the result of a shot from a twelve-bore double-barrel shotgun. You couldn't help but stare at it. This was one of the reminders of just how dangerous it could be, working in the kind of world my dad worked in. This particular battle scar was from when someone tried to shoot him while he was working on a door. My mum always said it was a contract shooting. The gunman was on the back of a motorbike; they shot him through a glass door. The other doorman working that night fell all the way to the bottom of the stairs of the basement club.

When the ambulance crew arrived, they went straight past my dad down the stairs and started to attend to the other doorman. In the meantime, Dad hailed himself a cab while bleeding profusely from his backside, and nonchalantly sauntered into Barts hospital, scaring the night staff to death with his 'Aris' half blown off. It was not just a straightforward trip to hospital; the police were asking a million questions. Also, Dad had to have surgery to get the shrapnel out of his wound.

As it turned out, my dad had to stay in hospital for a couple of days after the surgery. A nurse would have to pack out the wound with gauze and clean it thoroughly with surgical spirit. He played merry hell in that hospital, fooling around, playing tricks and pranks on the nurses and the other patients – they discharged him early because he was so destructive. Mum was well pleased with the result; nevertheless she did have the role of cleaning and packing out my dad's arse – he thought that farting was hilarious every time she was trying to pack it out, which gives you a little taste of what Dad was like.

I was asleep in the downstairs bedroom in Avenue Road. Now, Avenue Road was a big house, but it only had two upstairs bedrooms, and the only toilet in the house was downstairs. Because of his size, Dad could not fit into the single bed that Mum had downstairs – well, to be fair, he took up most of the double bed upstairs too. Jamie was staying with us at the time in the other upstairs bedroom. All of a sudden we heard a crash, bang, wallop on the stairs. Obviously I was thinking to myself, 'Oh my God, Dad has just fallen down the stairs!' I was too scared even to come out of my room, terrified at the thought of what I was going to find, because, you see, my downstairs bedroom door was directly facing the bottom of the staircase. If I opened the door, I would find Dad lying there in a heap. I could not bring myself to do so. However, I gathered enough courage and opened the door. Now, I know this will sound bad, but what a relief it was when I finally plucked up enough courage to open my door. To my astonishment, Dad was not lying on the floor at the bottom of the staircase – oh no, it was my brother Jamie instead.

'It's alright, Kel. I was half asleep. I thought I was at the bottom step and now I've fallen from top to bottom like a f**king *Starsky & Hutch* stuntman,' he said. With that, we both just burst out laughing.

All the way through his illness, Dad just loved talking about his own funeral. He would sit in the conservatory with his cup of tea in one hand, roll-up in the other, going, 'Val, come and take a seat here with me. Oh, and bring Kelly and Karen in with you too.' He would then proceed to quiz us constantly: 'Val, tell me what my funeral's going to be like? I want to hear all the details.' He also demanded that he didn't want a dry eye in the church – yes, he actually wanted everyone to be upset, sobbing their hearts out.

It seemed such a strange request, almost as if he was getting some sort of kick out of it. Once again, I think that the idea of people caring about him sent him soaring back to his tormented childhood again, a time when he was constantly belittled and put down, not to mention the physical abuse that he had been made to endure.

Mum was all over the place; her head was at boiling point. The pressure of this was too much; she regularly broke down in tears, and let's face it, who could blame her? She just could not work it out at all: 'Where the f**k is he coming from, why does he insist on talking about his funeral in so much detail?' she would say.

It was incredibly hard for my mum to have to listen to her husband of thirty-odd years – a forty-nine-year-old man in the prime of life – going on and on about his impending death. He just would not let up. She was growing so tired of it; you would hear her repeatedly say to my dad: 'Len, you are going to have the best money can buy. You will have a horse-drawn carriage with four plum-coloured horses; the coffin will be covered in flowers; there will be a procession of twenty cars following you up. As you travel to the church, the pavements will be full of people paying their respects. There will be a police escort all the way to the cemetery, stopping all the traffic.'

Then Dad would tell her not to waste money on his funeral, but Mum would say that he deserved nothing but the best and there would be thousands of people showing their respect, absolutely thousands! With that, he would sit there grinning like the Cheshire f**king cat, happy knowing that his funeral would indeed be massive, in his words, 'a showstopper'.

My dad would say to my mum: 'I don't want to leave you, Val. What am I going to do without my Val?' He didn't seem to grasp that the fact of the matter was that he was the one leaving us, he was the one dying. The truth was that within the next six months, maybe even sooner, he would be gone: he would finally be out of pain and at peace. It would be us, the family, who would have to rebuild our lives, who would have to come to terms with the reality of living without my dad, 'The Big Guy'. As much as he drove us all mad at times, he was still our dad and Mum's soulmate and husband.

'What are we going to do without Len?' It was the question we were all agonising over.

So the days were flying by now. Isn't it funny, when you want a day to go slowly then it seems to go so very quickly, and when you want it to go fast, it drags along like a wounded snail? Every day that came and went was another day closer to that dreaded day. Talking about his funeral, day in and day out, did not help one bit; there was just no getting away from it at all, no escaping the by now inevitable.

As most of us do at times such as these, we all tried to remain upbeat and to carry on as if everything was all OK, when in fact the cancer was not just killing my dad, it was killing a part of us all. In fact, the only person it did not seem to be getting to was the one person who was suffering with the illness. Being a proud man, as indeed my dad was, if he was worried about his death then he certainly did not show it to us. As the cancer progressed, his book signing at Dillons (now a Waterstones bookshop) in Tottenham Court Road was due. His book was yet another success story for him, like *Lock, Stock and Two Smoking Barrels*, which he would never have the good fortune to enjoy.

On the day of the book signing, my dad looked awful – all through his illness he never really looked ill. On this day he did. He didn't feel up for it, but like the true trooper he was, he put on his shirt and trousers and waited for the limousine to come and pick us up and take us to Dillons bookshop.

While we were on the journey to the signing, we had the usual interrogation: 'How many people will be there?' 'How many copies of the book will I sell?' 'How long will the queue be?'

'Len, don't worry, the queue will be out of the door,' Mum said.

As we approached the bookshop, we all got very emotional. I had a lump in my throat; all of us were choked at the sheer volume of people waiting to get a signed copy of my dad's book, *The Guv'nor*.

My dad broke the ice: 'F**k me, Val! How am I going to sign all those books?'

And then: 'What if I can't spell their names?'

And finally: 'I hope they've got enough copies of the book lined up in case I muck 'em all up!'

'Don't you worry about it, Len,' Mum replied. 'It will all be fine.' Ever the voice of reason, he listened to her every word. She could always calm Dad down and make him feel comfortable.

As my dad got out of the car he was mobbed by fans wanting to shake his hand and wish him all the best. It made him feel like a superstar for a few minutes, and for a short while the cloud over us was completely gone. There were no thoughts about the cancer and what was so very closely up ahead; we all enjoyed the moment for what it was: a fantastic achievement for my dad to be proud of.

Dillons was a large bookstore; it had a double-fronted

shop door in the middle, with two massive windows decorated on either side with huge posters of my dad's book cover. Inside the shop, there were a couple of steps leading up to a wooden desk at the back of the room; it was there that my dad and his co-writer Peter Gerrard sat, ready to begin the signing. Overseeing the day's events were Dad's great friends John 'The Neck' and Al Crossley – these two big powerful men were there to look after Dad, if you know what I mean!

In the queue, we recognised a few young faces and a few old characters who came along to support my dad. He immediately recognised one in particular. This kid was a bit of a tearaway when he was younger; he was one of Jamie's friends and mine too. He had about five copies of the book under his arm, all of which he wanted signing.

As my dad was signing the books for him, he said, 'Son, you make sure you pay for those books, you got it? Listen, boy, I'll be keeping a close eye on you!'

Old habits don't die…

'Of course I will, Len,' said the young tea leaf.

Although he was getting tired, due to the amount of time he had sat in one position, my dad continued to sign each and every book for his devoted fans. Every now and again he did lose concentration, though. We could see he was getting tired; he did not look that great and you could tell that it was taking its toll. Mum was very concerned about his health; all that he was concerned about was how many copies of his books he had sold. Dad had one eye signing each book and the other fixated on the f**king cash register! Every ka-ching that the till made was one more of his books sold.

Like a real man, no matter how ill Dad must have been feeling, he just sat at that desk with his pen at the ready and waited to sign every last book that landed on the desk in front of him. He made the odd joke too and painstakingly smiled for photos. Not one single person left that shop without a few words, a brisk handshake and a smile from The Guv'nor himself. We were so proud of him that day.

11

THE MORNING OF 28 JULY 1998

The McLean family household woke as normal. We had Dad's second book signing to attend, which was to be held in Liverpool Street Station. He was too ill to go, so Karen was going to stay with him while Mum, Jamie and I went. Mum was busy getting ready, Jamie was in the shower and I had to nip off to my flat. We all looked in on Dad, but he was sleeping, so we didn't disturb him. Sue, my dad's Macmillan nurse, was also there, as she stayed over some nights. While Mum was drying her hair, Sue went in to check on Dad and then came over to Mum and said, 'Val, Lenny's not going to wake up, he is in a semi-coma. He will hear everything you say to him, but he won't come out of this coma. Whoever you want here, call them now.'

Straight away, Mum phoned me: 'Kelly, don't panic, but you need to come straight home.'

That phone call haunts me to this day. I remember driving home sobbing, tears streaming down my face, thinking, 'Why, why, why my dad?' I pulled up on Mum and Dad's drive and ran straight upstairs to him.

Mum also rang Dad's brothers and sisters so that they could say their goodbyes too. Dad was lying there in the bed as Mum stood holding his hand, reassuring him that everything was going to be OK. His biggest worry was Mum, and how she was going to be, then of course Jamie and me.

I remember lying next to Dad, cuddling him and sobbing. The emotion in that room was so high – the man we all loved so much was about to leave us; we were about to experience the greatest loss of our lives. He was still holding Mum's hand with a really light grip for such a strong man: not wanting to let go, not wanting to leave us. Dad's brothers and sisters were downstairs in the conservatory.

Eighteen years on, Karen and I are writing this and the tears are rolling down our faces. The death of someone so close is a heartbreak that I guess we never get over.

My mum was crying, holding my dad's hands, rubbing one and telling him, 'It's OK, Len, go to sleep, the kids and I will be fine,' and with that Jamie threw himself on the bed, one arm over Dad, the other around me. Karen had her arm around Dad and the other was holding my mum. Dad's brothers and sisters came up to say their goodbyes and then went back downstairs. The four most important people in his life were left with him: Mum, Jamie, Karen and me.

Sue, the Macmillan nurse, said that Dad would be breathing heavily and the breaths would be longer – 'He will take a long, deep breath and you'll hear a rattle in his voice, and that will be his last breath,' she explained.

But Dad just kept breathing and breathing. Eventually, Mum said to him, 'Lenny, you need to let go, it's time, I love you.'

With that, my precious dad took one long, deep breath – and passed away. God bless him…

The emotion in Mum and Dad's bedroom was horrific – I don't think I will ever be able to express in words just how we all felt. Downstairs, I could hear one of my aunts talking to some male voices, voices I didn't recognise. I was clinging to my dad, not wanting him to go. Mum was in a bundle on the floor; Karen was holding her and they were both sobbing, while at the same time trying to console one another to no avail.

I heard footsteps coming up the stairs closer and closer to us. My poor, poor mum! Nothing I could say or do would help her. Mum, Karen and I left the room while the men from the funeral parlour got Dad ready. I remember being held by one of my uncles in the kitchen. From the kitchen I saw the men pass by with my dad. I ran straight upstairs, reached the bedroom and stared at the empty bed where he had lain. Then I walked over and lay in the same spot where he had just been. Lying in the same position he had been in, I just sobbed. I don't remember how long I lay there, but Mum came in after a while and we held each other in complete silence; it was truly devastating.

Throughout my dad's illness, he kept his strength, his pride and most of all his dignity. He remained a proud man, right to the bitter end.

* * *

As I'm sure you can imagine, on the morning of the funeral the mood was so sombre; none of us had wanted this day to come. To be honest, a lot of that day was a complete blank to me – I was concentrating on looking after Mum and getting her through the day. I just wanted the funeral to be over with; I wanted to go home, to a place where we alone could comfort one another, together as a family unit, knowing that we were all feeling the exact same emotions. Mum was sitting in a chair frozen, waiting to bury my dad, her life and her love since the first day they met when she was just seventeen years old.

As the cars pulled up, I saw the flowers: they were amazing, he had so many. Mum sent: 'Len, love you always, your Val.' I sent: 'To Daddy, love Kelly.' Karen got a double-heart that was put at the back of Dad's coffin. Mum said, 'That's exactly where he would want Karen.' Then there was Daddy Cool: 'Privileged to have known you,' with a black suit jacket, boxing gloves and even the front cover of Dad's book, *The Guv'nor*.

I went to find Mum and tell her the cars had arrived.

'I can't do it,' she said.

I put my arms around her, lifted her out of the chair and said, 'Come on, Mum, we can do it, this is the last thing we can do for Daddy.'

The next thing I can remember is being in the car following my dad's coffin – he was aged just forty-nine and in the prime of his life. It just wasn't right, it wasn't fair at all. There were so many black cars and hundreds following as we turned onto the motorway. I looked behind us: oh my goodness, I couldn't believe it, the cars went on for miles and miles!

The police had blocked the roads and they were standing with their hats off, showing their respect. We had a police escort all the way to the crematorium. It was such a sad, sad day, but I was so proud, as there were *Lock, Stock* film posters on every billboard along the journey. Dad was literally looking down on his own funeral, just as he wanted, just the way he had spoken about it, and just how he had pictured every moment of this day, over and over. He had basically lived it with the biggest smile on his face; he would have been so proud to know how much he was loved – and not just by his family.

The pallbearers said afterwards that Dad's coffin was the heaviest they had ever carried and the biggest as well. At the end of the service, the priest said, 'Everyone is welcome back at Val's.' You should have seen my Mum's face! There were hundreds and hundreds of people there. He was supposed to say, 'Family and close friends are all welcome.'

Mum's house was packed with so many people; her garden was packed too. There were some mourners that we had never even met before.

The last person must have left around three in the morning, and at that point, Mum, Karen and I cleared up and went off to bed. We had had a few drinks down us, so that over the process of the night, we actually got a little sleep. It was such a draining day and a very long, traumatic one at that.

12

JUST ONE MORE DAY

A feeling that I am sure most families out there who have lost such a close family member can relate to is that wrenching feeling of complete and utter loss. Day-to-day life as you know it seems to come to a complete standstill. Nothing matters anymore, you just feel completely numb. The world seems hazy, as you walk around in a total daze. The idea of never seeing that person again, the very thought of it being forever permanent, is so heartbreakingly final. Nothing else can be done to help them, no more new memories will ever be made.

The three of us, Karen, my mum and I, slipped into a mild bout of depression. We slept a lot – I guess this was the body's way of coping. We were forever looking at one another for some sort of answer. One thing I did keep saying to my mum was, 'Mum, I just want one more day with Daddy.'

'Why, Kelly, why do you want one more day?' she would reply. To which I had no answer, except, 'I suppose, if any such wish could ever have been granted, I would have asked for the same wish every day of my life. Every waking day until the day that I myself passed away.'

To this day, I still have the same recurring thought; I still feel the same way as before: one more day. One thing that has always puzzled me is that I have never had that thought of needing one more day with my mum. Of course, I wish she was still alive today; that's a given. But I had a very different relationship with her to the one that my dad and I shared. She and I were like soulmates, the best of friends. We could, and would, talk about anything to one another. Mum and I had a very special connection indeed, so much more than just mother and daughter.

The relationship I had with my dad was completely different: we clashed a lot, my dad and me. I think we were simply too much alike. As I have said previously, when my dad was a young man growing up, most of our family and the public alike disliked him with a passion, simply because of his attitude. He had a terrible temper, he did not give a f**k for one single person, he would act on impulse and he would never take a step back and try to deal with a certain situation in a different way. Empathy was not a feeling that he could ever produce. No, he would just react in the only way he knew how, the only way at his young and impressionable age he ever felt comfortable with – and that, of course, was extreme aggression. A belt in the earhole or a toe in the bollocks would be the order of the day. And because of this, and rightly so, many people judged him on that, and that alone. I mean, can you really blame them? This was the only Lenny McLean they ever knew. Now I have to confess that I too was one of those people who judged him, one of those people who did not like him. Listen, as difficult as this is for me to admit, I would even go so far as to say that at times I absolutely hated my dad, and that for me is one heartbreaking fact!

For the last twenty years since his death, I have had to live with the fact that I harboured thoughts of hatred towards my dear departed dad. I have constantly regretted having those thoughts in my head and the way I looked at him with undisguised hatred in my eyes. I'm appalled by the fact that I too judged him along with everybody else. How judgemental must I have been? Nevertheless, as we all know, hindsight is a truly remarkable thing. Because as I reflect on my own experiences in life, what I now know is that unbeknown to me, and for so many years, I adopted the self-same philosophy that my dad did in the way that I dealt with the day-to-day things as I went through life – a 'hit now and take questions later' kind of approach – and for this reason alone, people have constantly judged me.

I have argued and fallen out with friends and family and the people I love and care for the very most. Just like my dad, I had a very bad attitude, and a raging quick temper to go with it. On the surface, to everybody looking in, I didn't give a flying f**k about anyone. Outwardly, it would have seemed as though I really did not, but deep inside, it was destroying me. And at a time when I was trying so hard to work through my issues, when I so desperately needed the support of the people around me, I felt rejected by my outer family (by that statement, I think you know just who you are). It is all so apparent to me that like my dad, I too am misunderstood, and as a result simply written off as one of life's bad eggs.

But this is not the case; I just see the world differently to most people. Unless you can accept the fact that I am in some ways different, then there will always be a problem. Yes, I am trying to think differently every day, trying not to react immediately and trying to take time out to think about my responses. And I am now getting the help that I need for my condition. The help that sadly was not available for my dad to take advantage of when he was alive.

As I said earlier, hindsight would have been a wonderful thing in my case, and it might have changed my relationship with Dad, maybe even saved my sanity. It could have also saved me from those recurring negative thoughts that were running around my head. If I had known then what I know now, what I've learned over the past two years, it could have saved me from hitting an all-time low.

You see, I was referred to a mental health expert, who has been assessing me for the past two years. The conclusion made by my GP was that I am suffering from a debilitating condition (I will explain this in more detail later in the book). However, taking medication and working on my thought processes on a daily basis is helping me to lead a much more normal and stable life, a life that my dad was never able to live.

In writing this part of the book, I am fast learning that for all of those years that I spent beating myself up over thoughts that I needed just one more day to put things right between my dad and me, I now know, for the record, that I did not. Because at that time in his life, essentially he seemed to have been suffering from the self-same condition. In addition, and worst of all, I have been given a second chance to live a normal life, a life without chaos running through my head: a peaceful serenity. A life that my dad would have loved, but simply never had the chance to live.

Therefore, Mum was right all along. One more day would never have helped me; I would not have been happy one bit! I would have wanted more and more every time because it just would not have been sorted out in that time, it might have taken a whole lifetime. There's one thing I could have said, though, and that is this: Dad, I am truly sorry that I ever judged you. I now understand the reasons why you acted the way you did.

At this time I could not bring myself to leave my mum's side – she was my safety blanket, and I felt truly safe with her. Nothing would happen if she was close by. I could stay in the background and let her do the upfront bit and deal with all of the sh*t by herself. That way, I could simply deal with Dad's death in my own way. I was also trying to fill a void, trying desperately to fill the massive hole left by his passing.

Karen and I carried on living with my mum. As I just said, I did not want to leave her side – we did everything together, it was always the three of us. Before we knew it, the weeks had turned into months; we had shut ourselves away from the world outside. Mum spoke to a few close friends and family who would ring the house to see how we were doing, but other than that, we had no contact with the outside world. I completely hid myself under the radar and slipped into a terrible depression. At this point, I began to self-harm, usually by cutting myself, or picking at my head and skin until it was raw – I suppose it was a cry for help.

My mum quickly noticed my mindset – she could quite easily see, as it was evident in my actions. Now she didn't just have to deal with the loss of her soulmate and husband, oh no, she had a performing Kelly to deal with too. It was a dreadful time, and due to the depression, anxiety and grief surrounding my dad's death, my weight plummeted to a devastating degree.

As a teen, I had suffered with anorexia, a debilitating mental anguish which I dealt with alone. As I really did not know who to ask for any kind of help, I would stop eating or self-harm as a way of letting people know that I needed help. I now know that this is not the way to ask for help, but rightly or wrongly, it was my way; I could also punish myself for what had just happened. Looking back, it is a punishment that I have always unleashed on myself my entire life.

In a strange way, in my head, this was a way of helping Mum. Deep down, I thought that if she was worried about me and all of my problems and issues, it would help take away the pain that she was feeling with the recent loss of my dad. All of her time and all of her thoughts would be geared towards looking after me, getting me back on the right road. However, as I look back, I simply think how selfish I was then. I played it completely wrong and I wish I could tell her how sorry I am. Once again she had to deal with another problem. All of her life she had had to deal with the sh*t that my dad and I brought to her door. She tried to draw me away from my depression: 'Kelly, you need to get out of the house, you need to break away from me and get your life back on track!' she told me. 'None of this is your fault, you didn't cause Daddy's death. Why don't you get yourself a job? Listen to me, Kelly, you should start getting back to the real world, start communicating with people once again.'

All of her ideas were completely on point, but the problem was that I just did not feel ready – I simply could not be bothered to do anything at all. So in order to please my mum, I just went along with her, but unbeknown to her, I did not intend to take any of her solid and positive advice. You see, what many people are not aware of is that a person with my kind of mental illness is as cunning as a lighthouse rat. We can manipulate any given situation to get what we want, or at least at the time, that is what we truly believe. However, looking back, I'm really not so sure.

I think deep down my mum knew exactly how my head worked; she was playing a game, just as much as I was. It is simply me being Kelly McLean – I am stubborn beyond belief, and once I get my mind set about something, there's no way on this earth that anyone is going to change it. This is another similarity that Dad and I shared. He too was as stubborn as a mule; it would always have to be his way or no way at all. You see, with my situation back then, Mum would just be planting a certain seed, a seed that I would have to water in the hope of making it grow.

One morning, as we were just waking, the landline was ringing. Mum got up and answered: it was my great-aunt, Rita Ruddock. Rita invited my mum to go over to Bethnal Green to her house. Funnily enough, it's the exact same place where she still lives to this day. Anyway, Aunty Rita suggested that Mum went down to Bethnal Green Market and had a spot of lunch; she also thought maybe she should spend the night at her house. However, as I said earlier, me being a cunning little f**ker with multiple issues, I just knew that this was a set-up to split my mum and I up, to break the emotional umbilical cord that I had been using like a parachute.

I still speak with Rita on a daily basis. After my mum's death in 2007 she inadvertently took on the role of a surrogate mother to me. She was always willing to listen to me and still is today if I need a little guidance. Aunty Rita is always there to give me some good old-fashioned, old-school East End advice, straight from the hip and no pulling punches – she says it how it is. So anyway, Mum decided to take Rita up on her offer and left me to fend for myself.

On their trip down Bethnal Green Market, they bumped into an old friend of Rita's, a woman called Doreen. Now, Doreen owns a pub along the Mile End Road called the Bancroft Arms. My family has always seen the Bancroft as a proper drinkers' pub, a boozer filled mostly with men who go straight from work for a few pints and a good old East End chinwag with their pals. None of this glass of wine cobblers where you sip for an hour until it's drunk. No, it's a fully-fledged geezers' boozer, full of the stench of toil and sweat from an honest day's graft. I'm sure you all know the sort of pub I'm talking about.

Anyway, Rita introduced my mum to Doreen, and while they were chatting, she asked her if she needed any bar staff.

'Why, Val, do you want a job?' Doreen enquired.

'No, not for me, Dor. It's for my daughter Kelly, she hasn't left the f**king house since my Lenny died!' Mum replied.

'Well, as it goes, Val, I could really do with someone to do the lunchtime shift, if that suits?' said Doreen.

So, when my mum returned home the next day, she told me about her meeting with Doreen and about the job offer at the Bancroft, to which I immediately said, 'Mum, I'm not ready!'

'Kelly, please try it out,' Mum asked. 'Please do it for me, babe. I really do need you to do this, and look, if you don't like it then you can always leave, eh?'

Obviously, I knew she was right: I had to get motivated again. So I agreed to give it a go.

My first couple of shifts at the Bancroft were a little nerve-racking, to say the least. I was a bit withdrawn. However, as time went on, I became more and more at ease. I must say, my mum was 100 per cent right, and after a short while, I actually began to enjoy myself. The job started to take my mind off my dad, and in parallel to that, my poor head was getting a bit of a rest too, a well-deserved break from negative thoughts. I even managed to break out into a smile now and then too.

For me, being around people in the pub who were

not emotionally attached to my family helped me out of my depressive state a great deal. Also, I had a flat round the corner from the pub that I had not stayed in for months, and with my confidence growing, I found that I could manage to stay there on an odd night too.

I must just say that I had a funny relationship with Doreen; it was one of those love-hate relationships. One minute we were screaming at one another, the next we were laughing and joking as if we were great pals. To be honest, I think that the two of us being East End girls through and through helped a lot.

In the coming few months, things became a bit easier – they do say time is a great healer. My negative thoughts became less frequent, but certain records or songs would come on the television and trigger something off, and then everything would come flooding back and knock me sideways. I suppose I was kidding myself if I thought I was OK.

For the most part, I was coming to terms with the reality that my dad would never come back, but was I truly taking it on board? I'm not so sure. I didn't deal with my emotions. Instead I was very cunning, adept at hiding most feelings away from the outside world. In my head it was just chaos, thousands of regrets, and guilt – why this, why that? – all mingling in a mass of mixed-up emotion. All of those thoughts

I securely locked away in my head, out of reach to anyone.

Over the years I have become top-class at hiding away my thoughts, putting up a barrier and wearing that all too familiar game face to the world. To this day, I'm still running my life in the same way, hiding my true feelings, putting up barriers. I only let the world see one side of me, the hard face – an 'I'm alright, Jack' kind of image. Deep down, I'm not sure if, in reality, I am winning the battle – I have a few good weeks, followed by a couple of bad ones. In life I find people always remember the bad and forget the good; we should spin this around and focus more on the good. I'm sure the world would be a much better place to live.

So I noticed that my mum's manner was changing, and I felt she was a lot more relaxed. She could see that I was getting my life back on track – well, on track in my world. I was mucking about, smiling; I enjoyed the little job I had and she did not have to worry about me.

Unbeknown to Mum, this was all an act. You see, it was all for her eyes only. In life, we are all acting out parts; there are certain scenes we have to play and we are far more adept at acting out some of these than others. My performance with regard to seeing my mum happy worked an absolute treat. An Oscar-winning performance, if I do say so myself, and the goal of seeing her a little happier again had finally been accomplished.

I noticed that soon after the workers had left the Bancroft, the evening's clientele changed somewhat to a bunch more befitting my mum's age. On a Friday night, a live band would take to the stage, performing a repertoire of old classics – mind you, a 'dead' band would be no good at all, now would it? All jokes aside, this encouraged me to start going down there a little bit myself too. So I would tag along with Mum, and by doing this, maybe I would have a chance of dishing out to her a little advice of my own. She met and became friends with some nice people. So with this in mind, I hatched a plan to try and get her to go alone. What I would do is this: I would let her get all ready to go, then just before the cab pulled up outside the house, I would make up an excuse that I could not go. As the driver was tooting his horn, I would say to my mum, 'You're all dressed and ready now, Mum. You might as well go on your own. All of your friends will be down at the pub anyway.' My plan worked, and from then on, she started to go to Doreen's on her own. I would just make my own arrangements from that day forward.

I could see over time that my mum's confidence

had started to grow back. She seemed to be a different person; she simply could not wait for her Friday nights out. During the week, she would go out shopping for a new outfit to wear, and she would never miss her Friday night out again.

At this point, I was controlling my demons a bit better too. Controlling them in the only way I knew how, and that was by crying for a few seconds and then slamming that emotional door firmly shut for another day. Of course, I would play up as if I hadn't a care in the world in the public's view, but deep inside I was broken.

I was in tatters and life was about to get worse. There was one Friday night that sticks in my head for obvious reasons that I will explain. As usual, my mum was in Doreen's with her new friends, and so I thought it might be nice to surprise her – you know, mother and daughter having a little drink together. However, to my astonishment, when I turned up it was not just Mum who was in for a surprise. Oh no! Unbeknown to me, I was in for the surprise of my life. You see, as I walked through the pub door and looked over to the left, I saw my mum's crowd. I discreetly stood back and watched her in the same way as you do your child without them knowing. Then I noticed this bloke standing very close to her. I could see immediately that there was some kind of chemistry between them, and knowing my mum as well as I do, it was clear to me that the two of them were far more than just friends. Abruptly, I made my way over to speak to her.

'I need a word with you outside, now,' I ordered.

So we went outside and I told her that I didn't like the way it was looking between her and this strange man. 'What's going on with the two of you?' I demanded. See, that's the old Kelly McLean – jump in and open my mouth to cut to the chase. Mum said that there was nothing going on, she said they were just friends, and had been out to dinner a few times. Now my mind went up a few gears and I wanted to know when, where... every last detail. How *dare* she! Immediately I felt betrayed, let down and angry.

'OK, so if you two are just friends and there's nothing more to it than that, why the big f**king secret?' I asked.

'Listen, Kelly, I didn't want any aggravation,' she said. 'If I had told you, I just knew that you wouldn't understand. I knew that like your dad, you'd simply just fly off the handle without giving me a second of opportunity whatsoever to try to explain.'

But I could tell by the look on her face that she was holding something back, and my mind now slipped into complete overdrive: 'I can't deal with this, Mum. Daddy didn't ask to die, he didn't want to have cancer… How could you do this to me?' I yelled. At this point I know exactly what you're thinking, and yes, I would seriously agree today: how selfish of me. But as I have explained previously, this was the type of person I was back then.

Looking at my mum I noticed a tear welling up in the corner of her eye.

'Kelly, no one will ever take Daddy's place. He's just a friend, it's just a bit of company, and you have no idea how lonely it has been for me being all alone without your dad.'

But before she had a chance to finish, I dismissed everything she had tried so hard to explain and stormed off. I then progressed to the next phase of my attack, and that was to lock myself away, bottle up my emotions and allow negative thoughts to take a hold of my imagination.

Over the next couple of days, Mum tried to phone me about a million times, but I simply could not answer. Every time I saw her number come up, I would immediately burst into tears. All I could see in my head was this fella and my mum standing together, laughing and having fun at the bar, to a backdrop of my dad all alone and dead. It brought the memories of him flooding back, with a rawness as strong as it was on that dreadful day when he left this world.

Once again, there was no way I was ever going to accept this. I was trying to run the show, how *dare* my mum find a bit of happiness with someone else! She needed to be loyal and stand by my dad, and this for me was totally and utterly unacceptable. As I said to myself over and over again, 'I'm not having this!'

Soul-destroying as it was, I was unable to speak to her. My mind was set: I was determined to put a stop to this friendship, no matter how my mum saw it.

Once again, the default mode in my brain took over and I dealt with it in completely the wrong way. Yes, I had lost my dad, but she had lost her husband, the man she had created a family with, the man she had loved for the best part of three decades. I mean, it couldn't have been easy for her to move on, now could it? When I mull it over in my head, I can see where she was coming from. Thinking about her sitting alone, night after night in front of the TV... It must have felt like some kind of hell on earth after having my dad around for all of those years.

But I went into child mode and decided that I wasn't going to speak to my mum, in the hope that maybe this would stop her from seeing this man altogether. Really, this was a way of me asking her to choose between him and me. It sounds as though I was completely jealous and that I wanted my mum all to myself, but this was simply not the case. The thought that kept running around my head every second of the day was that my dad did not hate life, he didn't commit suicide, he was just taken away from us because of a cruel illness. I guess I felt deep down inside that he had more to live for in life than the rest of us.

Let me explain... Life had dealt Dad such a bad hand – he was subjected to one hell of a gruesome childhood, and from such a young, vulnerable age, left alone to fight off a tirade of abuse and other sh*t. The physical side, he learned to deal with, but the number of mental issues that he had been left burdened with were just too complex for him to understand. Then just as his acting career was about to take off, and Mum and Dad were finally on the pathway to enjoy some of life's cream, he was cruelly taken away from us in a heartbeat.

I think to myself, 'Was any of this my mum's fault?' and immediately answer that question with an emphatic 'No!' However, once again she had copped the lot. I did not speak to her for a couple of months and for the first time in her life, she was not going to give in. Something changed in her after my dad died; maybe she just realised how quickly life can be taken away. It was so important for her to do what she wanted to do. I mean, when all was said and done, it was her life, not mine. I knew I had no choice; my plan had failed and now it was time to come to terms with the fact that my mum was in a new relationship, and this was how things were going to stay. It was either that, or simply risk losing my precious mum for good, I thought.

Nevertheless, in my head, it was still really him or me, even though I knew that for all of Mum's life she had put our needs and wants to the fore. Because in the past, her entire role in life was to look after my dad, Jamie and me. She must have thought to herself, 'No, bollocks, it's time to do what I want to do! I don't care what everyone else thinks,' and with a tear rolling down my face, I can say now, God bless you, Mum, and good on you!

Rather reluctantly, over the next few months, I started to get to know the man that my mum had chosen to have a relationship with, and it was par for the course that I would instantly begin comparing him to my father – that's just human nature, eh?

Right, so just to tell you a little bit about this fella that Mum was seeing. Tony was his name, and he was the complete opposite of Dad. I have tried to build up a picture of my dad throughout this book, so now let me build up a picture for you of Tony.

Tony was a London black cab driver, a calm and

softly spoken man. He was more of a modern man, the kind of fella who would take as long as my mum would take while getting ready for a night out. Whereas my dad... well, he was the complete polar opposite: sh*t, showered, shaved and dressed in the time that it took Mum just to put on her lipstick. Also, Tony was definitely not the kind of man who would want to be centre stage in front of a crowd, attracting all kinds of attention. However, it takes all kinds, and Mum and Tony just seemed to click. I think the sad fact that he had lost his wife to cancer a few years earlier, in a similar way to Mum losing Dad, was a big thing that they had in common with one another; although it was of course a very sad thing, I truly believe that this alone ignited their fondness for each other. I can imagine it helped the pair of them come to terms with it, having both been through such a tragic life experience.

As time went on, I was able to understand the reason for Mum's reaction when I first approached her about Tony. Obviously, the more I myself came to terms with it, the more I could see her point of view. Maybe I had been a little hasty, and indeed now I can see the reasons why she might want a companion. I mean, I can admit this to myself now, because now I know that my first judgement was completely and utterly wrong.

I had let the emotional part of my brain take over and subsequently make my decision for me.

Once I'd given Tony a chance and got to know him a little better, I found that he was a very nice man indeed. Let's face it, this man made my mum happy, and at that point I would even go so far as to say that I was pleased she had met him. He was a very nice man – what you saw was what you got – and if I'm brutally honest, I don't believe there are too many men like Tony out there. Now, don't get me wrong, sometimes he drove my mum mad – I know she had her moments too – but as we all know, not a soul among us is perfect. One thing that I would like to think is that if my dad had been looking down on us all then he would have been happy for her. Happy in the knowledge that she had found a companion as steadfast as Tony. He was a staunch and honest fella who would never have brought an ounce of trouble to our door, of that I am 100 per cent sure, not in a million years. Now my mum had a newfound chance of some kind of happiness, I thought maybe it was my turn: could I turn a corner and do the very same thing?

13

A BITTERSWEET
SYMPHONY

It was at a bar in Mile End in 2001 that I met the love of my life, Scott Richardson. Scott's friends would drink in the bar at lunchtimes, and one time he was there with them. There was an immediate connection when we met, and I instantly felt comfortable around him. Now, Scott is a real man's man, and let me tell you, this fella really did change my life with his good old-fashioned morals. He was a grafter and a provider. We were only together a few months when we decided to travel to Australia together. You see, we were sort of treating this little adventure as a make-or-break thing.

So here I was in my new relationship, starting a fresh new chapter in my life, with my mind firmly set on making it work. As I have said previously, I am very good at switching myself off, be that in a good or bad way. I can apply this whenever the mood takes me. I am not very good at dealing with the bad thoughts, though – I just lock all of that away for a little while to the far-off recesses of my mind, and before I know it, I'm back in that dark place of depression and low self-esteem once again.

I made a massive effort to hide that side of my personality from Scott, for he was a solid man – I didn't want him to run a mile. Once again I was hiding aspects of myself from the world. Scott saw half of me: the good half. Then again, isn't that true the whole world over? You highlight the good in you and try to cover up the bad? At the start of our trip, we had planned to stay Down Under for six months. However, I missed home terribly and this was the first time in my life that I was going to be away from my mum for such a long period. She wasn't going to be just a short drive away anymore; I wouldn't be able to drive over if Scott and I had an argument. It was time to grow up, and fast. I now had to think for myself and deal with certain situations as they arose all by myself. In addition, every time I phoned home, which was a hell of a lot at the start, Karen would get on the other end of the line and repeatedly tell me just how much she was missing me. So there we were, both crying our eyes out. 'Why don't you come home, Kelly?' she kept saying. To be honest, in light of recent events, I think that it was all just too much for her.

So I was calling Karen at all hours, crying, and she felt my pain and just wanted me to come home. The poor cow didn't sleep a wink, her eyes were black as coal. My mum said, 'Stop calling Karen crying, she's walking about like a zombie!' That made me laugh. I didn't give a thought to the time difference, and when it was 2pm in Australia, it was 2am in London. I tried to hide my emotions from Scott, and he usually wasn't next to me when I was on the phone to Karen. Even then, we weren't in each other's pockets, and we appreciated that we both liked our own space sometimes. However, he could tell I wasn't myself: 'Give it time, Kel,' he would say. 'It's all new, give it time, it's going to be an experience of a lifetime.' Somehow I managed to pull myself around, although the thirty degree heat and constant sunshine definitely helped!

Scott and I had a fantastic time in Australia, starting on the west coast in Perth. We then flew over to the east coast, a seven-hour flight. We stayed in Melbourne before driving down to Sydney. Then we drove up the east coast, stopping along the way until we reached Cairns – the trip from the bottom of Australia to the top took us five months.

Scott and I bonded, but I knew we were going to be OK. Normally, after a couple of weeks, people can't wait to run away from me! That man must have had the patience of a saint to have handled five months – I didn't want to let him go.

When Scott and I came home, he moved in with me straight away. Mum loved him and he loved her too. We had many great nights out together. Scott was an ideal son-in-law – hands-on with odd jobs, an area of Mum and Dad's relationship where Dad had never been useful, simply because she had done everything. Well, we thought Scott was hands-on, but then one day, Mum rang to ask him to fix a leak in one of her radiators. She ended up flooded and Scott was a plumber at the time! It cost her hundreds to get it fixed – mind you, he did try.

After a few years I said to Scott that I'd like a family. He agreed, and within weeks, I was pregnant. On 5 May 2006, our beautiful girls, Ruby and Prudence, were born. Boy, they changed our lives! Everything I could have wished for was right there. I was gutted my dad wasn't there with us; he would have adored them. All he ever wanted was to be a granddad, and he would have had one in each arm. Identical twins they were, and remain; they are everything to us, our world.

You can imagine Nana Val – she was besotted with them. They say twins are a gift from God. A new chapter was starting in our lives and it was so nice to see additions to the family rather than someone being taken away from us. In a perfect world, my dad would have been alive, and Scott's dad too. Scott's dad passed away in 2004, and I'm still sad that Prudence and Ruby never got to meet either of our dads, as I know the two of them would have made wonderful grandparents. But I know that they would not want us moping around all our lives. My dad would have said: 'Liven yourself up, enjoy yourself, but not too much (joke)!' Scott's mum, Silvie, became good friends with my mum, and she's always been a great help with the children and lended a hand when needed.

They were the next generation of the Richardson/ McLean household, and did my mum spoil them rotten. 'There's my Ruby,' she would proudly say, and I'd tell her, 'Mum, that's Prudence!' 'There's my Prudence,' she would say when she was holding Ruby – she never once got it right, bless her!

My mum could not wait until their first Christmas.

There were more presents for the twins – Christmas hats, babygros, etc – she would buy up the whole shop for the two of them if she could! Around the table on Christmas Day, we spoke about the future: birthdays, holidays, sleepovers at Nana Val's house when they grew older, that sort of thing. The twins did not have a clue: as the Christmas hats were miles too big for them, they were more interested in stopping them from covering their eyes.

A couple of months later, once again our happiness was taken away. Our family was once more in turmoil, because my mum had been diagnosed with lung cancer.

Mum's cancer was diagnosed just ten years after my dad had died, and it was yet another bombshell to deal with. 'What the f**k! Why is this happening to us again? How can life be so cruel? This world is such a cruel place at times,' I thought. And then, 'Why has it got to be my mum? All she's ever done is help people, she has never hurt anyone.' The news knocked the stuffing out of Mum. It was déjà vu, only this time it was not the three of us taking Dad to the hospital. No, this time there were only two of us taking my mum. So, was it going to end the same way, would it soon be just two? It was time to re-live the anguish all over.

We were back and forth to the hospital for

appointments, one after the other. Everything came flooding back like a tsunami, but I had to hide it from my mum. There was no way I was going to have her worrying about me. On the outside, strong, hard-faced; inside a crumbling wreck. I had one-year-old twin daughters, no dad, a mum with cancer and mental issues dating back to my childhood. Writing this piece, I have to give myself a pat on the back for getting through it all. Jamie and I never missed a hospital appointment with my mum. He and I took her for some tests and then we were back up the hospital for the results: they had seen a shadow on her lungs. The doctor said it was probably old scarring. 'Old scarring, that means she is going to be OK, right? There is a god after all,' I thought.

'Mum, you're going to be OK! Please promise me you will never smoke again,' I said.

'Kelly, another fag will never cross my lips,' she promised.

Mum would still have to have some more tests, but the worst was over, it seemed. Worst of it over, now that was a joke! At our next appointment with the doctor, all of our hopes were dashed. As soon as we sat down, I could tell by his face that it was going to be bad news: 'It's lung cancer,' he said. 'Probably scarring.' I chose not to hear that part of the report.

Mum looked at Jamie and me and said, 'I'm sorry.'

'*Sorry*? Mum, it's not your fault,' I told her.

I always thought my dad accepted his cancer like a man with dignity. Mum was very much the same; she was more worried about me than herself, which must be the parental instinct. For the next four months we were back and forth to the hospital for appointments, exactly as with Dad, ten years earlier. Then the appointments became more frequent, which we knew from experience to be a bad sign. Mum was given just six months to live in June 2007. From the October to her passing on 18 December that year, she spent the whole time in bed with us by her side.

Karen moved in for the last few months as my mum needed more and more help. There was no way we were going to leave her on her own. I would travel back and forth from Mum's – I wasn't able to move in with her as I had the twins to look after. It would not have been fair, moving in with one-year-old babies and all the noise and chaos that goes hand in hand with them; my mum needed peace and quiet.

I would park up on Mum's drive and she would tell me that Karen had just bathed her and that she had also just changed the bedcovers. See, the thing was, I couldn't bear the thought of my mum not washing and lying in dirty bedsheets. I would constantly be on her case: 'Come on, Mum! Let's get you up, wash you, and while you're up, I'll change the bedding.' But she was too frail to be pulled around. I am not the most dainty of people when it comes to that sort of thing either.

Anyway, as soon as I walked through the door, my mum would say, 'Kelly, Karen has just given me a bath and changed the sheets.' But I knew that she was lying. 'Mum, I'm going to change the sheets anyway,' I would tell her. Next, I got her over my shoulder, like in a fireman's lift. Opposite the bed, my mum had full-length mirrors on her wardrobe doors, and I could see from the mirror that she was pulling faces behind my back as if to say, 'Here we go again.' After I had finished washing my mum and moving her around, I would carry her back to bed, where the three of us would sit.

'Kelly, I know you mean well, but you're knocking the bollocks out of me! I'm shattered after you've finished pulling me around,' said Mum. For some reason the three of us would look at each other and just start laughing in a nervous way.

I tried my hardest to be a bit gentler, moving and pulling my mum around. But I refused to stop because I did not want her personal hygiene to suffer: she was always a very proud woman and she still had her pride and dignity. And so we continued this routine for the last couple of months of her life.

* * *

I got a early morning call from Karen: 'Kelly, you need to come over as soon as you can.'

'What's wrong?' I said as panic mode set in.

'Kel, your mum is in pain. She has asked me to call an ambulance for her.'

Unlike my dad, who was not afraid of dying, my mum was: she felt safer being in hospital with us around her. This was where she wanted to be when she would finally pass away. I knew in my heart of hearts that this was it: my mum would never come out of the hospital alive. She would never set foot back inside her house. I would never make her another cup of tea there... This was final.

I pleaded with Karen not to phone the ambulance, tears running down my face: 'Not yet, Karen. She won't come out of the hospital... I'm not ready to lose her yet.' Then I put the phone down, got in my car and started driving. I was in a zombie state, crying as I was driving. My tears were broken by the sound of my mobile phone ringing: 'Kelly, the ambulance has just arrived! Kelly, your mum was pleading with me to call them, she was crying with the pain. Meet us at Whipps Cross Hospital, the hospice department,' said Karen.

By the time I reached the hospice department, the nurses were just settling my mum down in her room. Straight away, she looked relaxed; she looked calm and contented. The fear had gone from her face, she did not look in pain anymore.

As soon as the nurses had finished, I started the interrogation – on and on I went. A little bit later, my dad's sister – my Aunt Boo – came to see Mum and we sat around the bed with her. This seemed to perk my mum up. She looked a lot better; she was sitting up, laughing and joking. Maybe I was wrong, she did need this little rest break. I know it sounds mad, but even though this was a hospice, getting her out of the bedroom where she had been stuck for the last couple of months was helping her.

She looked so good that Karen and I felt relaxed enough to leave her to rest for the night on her own – we felt she felt safe, she was not afraid and that she was going to be able to have a good night's sleep. We said our goodbyes that night in a different frame of mind; there was a glimmer of hope that the curtains weren't drawn completely shut, some light was getting through. You could sense the positivity in the room.

Karen and I stopped off and got a bottle of wine.

We had a nice night; we laughed and joked, thinking Mum was going to be alright. We finally got to bed at around 3am. I don't know if it was the drink or seeing my mum sit up in bed without pain or the glimmer of hope, but I slept like a baby. When I woke, I had a little bit of a hangover, but that was overshadowed by the positive thoughts regarding Mum.

Then the phone rang: it was Jamie. Every ounce of life drained out of me.

'Where are you?'

'We are getting ready, we won't be long – why?'

'Mummy's had a terrible night, she has not got any skin left on her elbows.'

I rushed to the hospice and headed straight for the nurse who was looking after my mum.

'Why the hell did you let this happen to my mum? I have looked after her for the last six months at home; for the last three months she has not been able to get out of bed! She has had one night here and she hasn't got any skin left on her elbows. Who was keeping a eye on her? I will tell you who: NO ONE!'

The nurse replied calmly, 'Kelly, we were keeping a eye on her, but we cannot allocate a nurse to be with your mum twenty-four hours of the day. She lies down and then she drags herself up by the elbows constantly. This is called "aggravated death".'

'So what are you saying? She won't be able to go home, she's going to die here too?'

Deep down, I already knew the answer, but I needed it to come from the nurse.

'Yes, Kelly. All we can do is try and make your mum as comfortable as we can.'

I just broke down; it was a waiting game and it wasn't going to be too long to wait. The next four nights, Jamie and I stayed with my mum – there was always at least one of us there with her, she was never alone. In secret, she had had pieces of jewellery made for us to keep as a memory, so she asked us to go in and accept her presents. She wouldn't let anyone in other than Jamie, Karen and me, but she made one exception: my partner Scott was invited in as she had had something made for him too.

The final days of my mum's life were quite surreal. My mum's partner, Tony, would come and sit with her, but in the final couple of days she would only let me, Karen and Jamie into the room. She was a very proud woman and wanted people to remember her before this horrible disease had taken hold. We took it in turns to sit with her, not that it was a chore. No, it just gave us a chance to sit back and reflect with her, and one by one to say our personal messages. One surreal moment I had while I was alone with Mum was when she asked me to move out of the way because my dad was standing behind me. I knew these were signs that time was running out for us to be together. It choked me up, but in a strange way, I was comforted, because by my mum seeing my dad, I knew that she wouldn't be on her own when she passed. Being on her own was one of Mum's greatest fears; my dad coming back to collect her put her at ease.

She went into a sort of comatose state and we were told by the nurses that she wouldn't wake up, but she could hear what people were saying to her. Jamie left the room to go and get us a coffee.

Karen and I were sitting next to her, talking to her on and off. The room had this eerie silence about it.

'Kelly!' shouted Mum, and then this eerie silence came over the room again.

I looked at Karen: 'Did you hear that?'

'Yes.'

'Don't worry, Mum. I'm here, I'm not going anywhere. We all love you deeply, but now it's time to go over and be with Daddy,' I told her.

Over the next few hours, Mum's breathing became very laboured and shallow. It was getting quite late at night. Jamie looked at me and said, 'Kelly, I don't want to stay in this room tonight, I'm going to sit by myself outside.'

I turned to Karen and said, 'Karen, do you mind waiting outside too? I just need to be with my mum alone.'

The nurses came in and made a put-up bed for me right alongside my mum. I leaned over and kissed her: 'It's just me and you tonight, Mum, I'm not going anywhere!' I said. I lay next to her, holding her hand. Eventually I fell asleep. I was woken by my dad's song, 'Daddy Cool', playing. This was the record that was played whenever he entered the ring for his boxing matches. Immediately, I sat bolt upright. Something drew my eyes to the corner of the room. There was a bright light and in that moment I realised that I was no longer holding my mum's hand. I leaned over and touched her hand: it was cold. Mummy had gone, and that was the reason why I'd heard my dad's song: he had come down and taken Mum away; they were finally back together again.

All alone, I lay next to Mum, cuddling her, crying. I wanted to spend a couple more minutes alone with her. Then I got myself together and called Jamie and Karen, who were both asleep outside the room. They came in and I said to my brother: 'She's gone, Jamie.' There we were, consoling each other at the loss of another parent taken from us so young. While my mum and dad of course weren't Karen's biological parents, she felt this loss just as much as we did. At least we could say that we had looked after Mum's every need right up until her very last breath. I was then the one who had to make the dreaded phone call to Tony at home in the middle of the night to let him know that Mum had passed away.

Heartbroken is an understatement: I was completely broken, a shadow of my former self. My life would never be the same again.

On Mum's deathbed, she told Karen: 'Love these girls like I myself would, please promise me that, Karen?' The very idea of leaving her beautiful granddaughters broke her heart, especially as they were still only babies, just eighteen months old. Mum bought all of the Early Learning Centre's toys, prams, everything, and at a time when they could barely walk. She wanted to see them with hair; she was devastated to leave them, they made her smile every day.

Karen promised my mum she would always love Prudence and Ruby as if they were her own, and that she would always be there for them no matter what happened, and she has kept that promise; she has never broken my mum's wish, not for one second. Karen is nan, granddad, aunt and uncle all rolled into one. The girls worship her, and let me tell you this, that girl has lived up to it all. She has been there every step of my girls' lives to this day, and will continue to do so; she is always there for the girls and me.

On Karen's fortieth birthday, my girls officially adopted her as their aunt. To Karen, this was better than receiving a million pounds. She was, and still is, over the moon with her official title. Karen never had children of her own and treats mine in the same way that my mum and dad treated her. Some people come and go, but Karen is part of the family and always will be.

14

LIFE AFTER

After my mum passed away, I no longer wanted to go on living in the East End of London with constant reminders of my childhood indoors. Mum had only lived about five miles away in Buckhurst Hill, and even though it was close by, it was a completely different atmosphere to what I was used to. The place felt a lot calmer, people would stop and say good morning to you in the street – what a difference to the East End. The only time people would talk to you there would be to ask if you had any spare change. It didn't smell stale; the air was fresh and clean. Life just seemed so much more relaxed. It was the sort of life that I wanted for myself, and quite honestly, a life that I needed, if not just for the sake of my sanity.

Unlike the East End, Buckhurst Hill didn't have problems such as drunken men and women screaming and shouting at one another down the streets at 1am every single night, or the mayhem when the local pubs were closing. Police helicopters would always be hovering overhead, and sirens ringing through the streets at all hours, day and night. Oh, and this was just the weekdays in the East End: the weekends were worse.

When my mum was alive, Scott and I would spend a lot of weekends with her simply to get away from all of the noise and chaos, and if she went away on holiday with Tony, we would look after her bungalow. It gave her peace of mind and gave us a break into the bargain. It was a nice little respite from the East End, a place where Scott and I could totally relax, because there was no way of getting a good night's sleep during the summer evenings with the windows open when we were at home. This wasn't because of the fear of getting burgled or anything like that, no, it was all down to the bloody noise of local lowlifes who only seemed to come alive at night. You would have no trouble sleeping during the day, owing to the fact that the local scum were asleep too, because not one of those lazy f**kers ever did a day's work. Nevertheless, with the windows shut tight, you didn't get much sleep anyway, cos it would be a hundred degrees and baking hot! You'd be sweating your bollocks off for most of the night.

In the seventies and eighties, when we were growing up, the East End was a different place, or was it just as bad then and we didn't know any different? In those days there were no police helicopters hovering overhead, but that wasn't because there weren't any kind of dodgy dealings going on. No, it was simply down to the fact that the constabulary didn't own one. And as for the Old Bill making home visits… well, it just wasn't as easy back in the day. People didn't have mobile phones and many people didn't even have a house phone to call the police anyway. And as far as phone boxes went, these were simply used like urinals for the drunks to take a p*ss in. So if a person wanted to urgently call the Old Bill, they'd have to run down the street to a neighbour's house to use their phone. So was life any better back then? Well, if I'm completely honest, I'm not so sure.

However, for me and Scott, everything was changing in the East End, and far too quickly for our liking. The old East End was dead and gone, and we simply had nothing of any value keeping us in the area anymore. So that was that, and we decided to make the big move and escape to the country in pursuit of a calmer and much more tranquil existence.

We started house hunting right away, and it didn't take us too long because we both agreed that the second house we viewed was definitely the one for us. We did our homework before making our final decision, buying a copy of the local paper to get a feel for what the area was like. The front-page headline news was:

'Graffiti on a Bus Shelter!'

There was a picture of the offence, displaying to all the extent of this heinous crime. We looked at each other and laughed out loud. For f**k's sake, if this was the front-page news, we couldn't wait to move in! This newfound haven couldn't be any different to where we were moving from, because back on our manor, if there was a murder down our street, it was lucky to make it onto page seven of our local news. We took a drive round to the local school to have a look. Scott went in to speak to the receptionist and ask a couple of questions. When he got back into the car, he was laughing.

'Kel, you're not going to believe this! I just asked the lady about space in the school and she said they are hoping to build more classrooms but the plans all relied on whether or not they would be approved planning permission.'

'"I'm sure you will get it," I said. "I mean, it's not like you're asking to open a strip club, now is it?"'

He went on to say that he had never seen someone go so red in all of his life. The lady was so embarrassed over this throwaway comment. Anyway, we put in an offer on the house and were thrilled when it was accepted.

Even though my mum and dad had both passed away, there was still an outstanding debt on the street that was handed down to me to collect. It was an ongoing debt from when my dad was alive, passed down to my mum and then subsequently me. You see, what people don't realise is that in my dad's world, a debt doesn't just die along with the person, it gets passed down the line. So, every week this man would put an envelope through my door, topped up with a little bit of 'Lenny McLean' interest, or 'a drink' as gangland Britain would refer to it. As it turned out, this man was a good painter and decorator, so I said that I would let him off some of the interest if he painted the house for me, which he jumped at without a second's thought. Before too long we were in our new house, with no need to decorate. Oh no, my son, that was all taken care of by the Lenny McLean legacy.

'Cheers, Dad! See, as you would say, I'm never off the f**king earhole!'

We moved in on a Friday – we did it at the weekend because it gave us the whole of Saturday and Sunday to get everything straight in the house. When the first night of us living there came along, it seemed strange, as it was a lot darker than the East End; also, there was no need to shut up the windows because it was almost silent outside. To be honest, if anything, it was too quiet for Scott – at first he found it very difficult to sleep at all there.

The funny thing was, even though I hated the East End, I felt like I was missing out on something. I had the urge to keep going back down there, although to my dismay, every time I went back, it felt filthy and a hell of a lot rougher than the previous visit. No sooner had I seen the Canary Wharf tower block, which was close to where we had lived, than I felt this deep anxiety kick in. Driving up the M11, getting closer to my new home, made me feel far more relaxed. I was starting to appreciate it, thinking to myself, why had it taken me so long to cut ties with the old East End?

Now I looked forward to returning to our new home after my East End holidays – to this serene countryside with its calming fields opposite our house, where sheep roamed freely. The scene was already set for a peaceful and tranquil life and it felt as though nothing on this earth could spoil it. Everything was positive, but could there be a negative lurking around the corner? Well, just maybe. Due to the difficult climate with regard to school placements at that time, I was less than optimistic about getting the twins settled in at school. But I was wrong, because a little while later, Prudence and Ruby got a start at the local nursery and I could not be happier. I made friends with some of the local mums and I also got to know the teachers. It was, and still is, a beautiful and close-knit little community.

Shortly afterwards, a job opportunity came up in the girls' school for the position of MDA – or to you and me, it's simply known as a mid-day assistant. This was in no way going to be a career move, but it fitted in very nicely with the girls' timetable. So my life was going along great – a nice house, nice little job, with a whole heap of new friends. Yes, you could safely say that life was good again, and we ticked along quite nicely for the next couple of years.

After my mum died, I went straight home and put a dinner on for the kids, blanked all of my emotions out and focused solely on my family. No time for all that grieving malarkey. I never shed another tear; my girls were eighteen months old when my mum died, no time for grieving. Just paper over the cracks, don't let yourself get upset: the twins needed me, full stop, I came second. That was until I slowly started going downhill – I lost my enthusiasm to go to work and was turning up late. Worse still, if I was too late then I just wouldn't go into work at all. Then in the midst of all that, an extreme bout of depression brought my self-harming to the fore again. I began to self-harm in places that no one could see. Afterwards, I would put a plaster over the wound, and if Scott spotted any signs of this while I was undressed and asked about it, I would simply say that it was a boil or something similar.

'So, Kelly,' I would ask myself, 'what exactly has caused you to spiral like this?' It became immediately apparent to me that everything I had suffered mentally over the past couple of years had only come about in the wake of the untimely deaths of my parents, and for that reason I would punish myself with self-harming. From the outside looking in, my life was relatively stress-free. I had a nice home, two beautiful children, my loving and loyal partner Scott, and a fantastic little job to boot. But with this newfound realisation, I would gladly have given all of this up and lived in a cardboard box, just to have my mum and dad healthy and back in my life again. My innermost feelings suggested to me that I did not deserve the life that I now found myself living at the expense of my parents losing theirs.

Like an addict, I just couldn't stop this uncontrollable urge to pick at myself. I would look in the mirror and think I could see something under my skin, then I would get a needle or the end of a sharp pair of scissors and proceed to pick the first layer of skin off until I made a hole that poured with blood. While I was doing this I had no pain, no feelings, not a single emotion in my body. I just wanted to pick and pick, with blood under my fingernails and my mind totally blank, standing in front of a mirror for hours, a gaping wound on my chest and a pile of blood-stained tissues screwed up and strewn across the floor. The only time I felt any pain at all was when I had finished picking, and that wasn't physical pain, it was mental pain. I then had to face my two young girls with plasters and battle scars, scars that unbeknown to their innocent eyes, I myself had caused.

So, I would wait for everyone else to go off to bed and then spend the rest of the evening with my new best friends:

The mirror, a needle and me.

Glancing in the mirror, I was confronted by a raving lunatic staring straight back at me. I simply could not help myself doing the inevitable, and there was no way I was going to ask for help.

After a solid night's picking, I would leave all of the blinds in the house down, and in the semi-darkness, I would get the girls ready for school. Dimming the lights in the front room, I would tell them I had a headache and the bright lights were hurting my head, in the hope that they would not see me properly and catch on. I would then phone one of the mums I had befriended and ask if they minded coming past my house and taking the girls to school. I would try and alternate who I rang as I didn't want to raise any suspicions, suspicions that could maybe set tongues wagging, bringing them to the conclusion that something was wrong. You see, word spread very quickly in our little village community. Scott was totally unaware of my antics: I would sleep in the spare room, he would then leave for work very early in the morning to beat the London rush hour, and to cover myself, I would just say that I didn't want to disturb him as he had to drive to London every day.

As soon as the girls left for school, I would go back to bed as I was completely shattered after my fun-filled night in front of the mirror. I would set my alarm clock to wake me up just before I had to pick them up from school. I would always turn up a little bit late so that

I didn't have to face any of the other mums. Cunning little f**kers, us addicts, now aren't we? This was to be my dark secret. Only myself, a needle and a mirror knew anything about it.

Gradually, Scott started to notice the changes in me. He could see that I was different – I became very quiet and I was constantly tired and making less and less effort with my appearance. I would deny that I had any sort of a problem. That was until I stepped it up a notch. Looking in the mirror one day, I thought I could see something on my face – a mark, a blemish, there was definitely a mark of some sort. My eyes were transfixed on it. I took hold of a needle and proceeded to burrow it under my skin and pick the mark off my face. As I started picking, the intensity would be so strong that I could not even blink. My eyes would immediately dry up, there was no emotion whatsoever. The only thought running through my head was to get this thing from under my skin.

I didn't feel any pain at the time – I guess I was just numb to it all. Unlike an alcoholic, who wouldn't stop until they collapsed or passed out, I was able to stop inflicting pain on myself. I would look at the time and realise I only had a couple of hours to correct the damage that I had done, and immediately I would commence with a strict cleaning regime.

I would start by dabbing talcum powder on the open wound to stop the weeping. Sometimes I would cover the wound with cream and put a plaster on top instead, although this would always be dependent on the state of my face. After that I would hold an ice pack over the affected area to try and calm it down, as it would be red raw and inflamed. But I wasn't a miracle worker – I only had a couple of hours to fix the damage I had caused before I had to pick up the girls from school. Only now, I had a major problem: the affected area couldn't easily be covered up with clothes, as it was on my face for all of the world to see. So, I simply caked my face full of make-up – that seemed to work!

All of a sudden, the area around the scar started to throb. This reminded me of what I had just done, and now, feeling guilty and ashamed, my depression kicked in full blast. So I dealt with all of this in the only way I knew how, with the only option I believed I had open to me. And that was to hide myself away under the duvet for a couple of days, or as long as it took until the affected area had calmed down.

While lying in my bed, I would drift in and out of sleep. When I was asleep, it was the only time that my mind could relax. Because while I was lying awake, I would be constantly beating myself up about the damage I had caused to my family, not to mention the

LIFE AFTER

I ended the session right there – I couldn't face any more, it had drained the life out of me. Immediately, I went straight home, taking myself off to bed to rest my head. That session brought up a whole heap of emotions of volcanic proportions – anger, hatred, regret and many other thoughts that I felt I had no control over.

By now at least I knew exactly how this therapy caper worked: that my next session would start where I had left off from the previous week. The entire week leading up to the next session was making me anxious about going back, as the very thought of trawling through the traumatic subjects that we had covered the previous week filled me with dread. But once again I summoned up the courage to go to the meeting. Deep down, I knew that I had to attend this particular session, especially if I was hoping to reap some sort of clarity, and in turn benefit from these completely terrifying therapy sessions.

As I predicted, we started off the session going over the previous week's work. We spoke about the strong family bond, etc, and she asked me why I got so upset – she said that she had also noticed how extremely angry I became. To be fair, I didn't think that she would have picked up on my anger as I'm an aggressive person anyway at the best of times.

I told her that my mum and dad had passed away at a very early age, a homicide as I saw it, all down to a measly box made of cardboard that contained cancer sticks.

'Both of my parents were heavy smokers,' I explained. 'They both died so very young and both from lung cancer, a cancer undoubtedly brought on through the act of smoking, something that I will never ever be able to accept, and most definitely something I will never be able to get my head around.'

'So, let's go back to your brother Jamie,' she said.

So I told her that my brother and I no longer talked and that it broke my heart each and every day. The pain that I suffered from the break-up of our sibling relationship was almost exactly the same pain as I felt and still feel from losing my dear mum and dad, although Jamie is fortunately still alive and well. I told her that deep down, I knew that the thing that had happened between us could never be resolved unless I was willing to forgive and forget and accept it. I would not be able to move on in my life, to forget and accept something that sadly, I was physically unable to, sad as that sounds. In my head I had accepted my fate, no matter how hurtful it was for me – I was just going to have to live with the hurt because the alternative was too great for me to take on.

LIFE AFTER

I came out of that session thinking to myself, 'Well, Kelly, that wasn't as bad as you thought it was going to be, now was it?' I was pleased that I'd gone, pleased that I hadn't bottled it and backed out. The other thing that was spurring me on was that I knew I only had two more sessions left to go. Was this the reason why I was feeling slightly more positive, or had I simply released a massive wrecking ball from around my neck? Well, whatever the reason, I could not wait for the next session.

The penultimate fifth appointment started quite differently. Here, we spoke about my life in the present. She asked about my partner and our twin girls, Prudence and Ruby... oh, and not forgetting my best friend and adopted aunt to my girls, Karen Latimer. The majority of the questions she asked me were of a positive nature. Perhaps this was her plan all along: build up to a crescendo by starting the sessions from a place so dark and damningly negative, then bringing my feelings out by swamping me with an uplifting thrust of quick-fire positives. At this point, I could not wait for session six to arrive.

We started this session where we had left off the first session, with the psychiatrist asking me the same set of random questions. To me, this seemed a bit strange, but I went along with it anyway. After I had given my answers, she asked me how I felt the previous session had been and wondered if the sessions had helped me at all.

I paused for thought while I ran over the sessions in my head.

'Well, session one was a little strange, because you threw a great deal of random questions at me that I must say seemed almost exactly the same as the questions you have asked me today,' I said.

'Kelly, these questions are very significant. This will all become clear when I explain them back to you at the end of this session,' she told me.

'OK! So, session two and three, I found raw and very emotional, the issues that we spoke about hurt me deeply. I do remember crying a lot through most of those sessions.' I was on a roll at this point and gave no pause for interruption but simply carried on: 'Session four, I was completely dreading, but strangely enough, my head felt a little bit clearer, and much to my surprise, I noticed that I hadn't shed a single tear throughout the session.

'Session five was very positive – it seemed to bounce along very well. You focused on the good things in my life: my children, my partner and indeed my friends. I felt very happy and content during, and at the close of, session five.

'It was very clear to me that in my first four visits to you, I would mentally tick off each session in my head as soon as the session had ended. Yet as I came away from my fifth session I had completely forgotten to tick it off. This has shown me just how positive it must have made me feel, and that I was finally reaping some therapeutic benefits, lifting my spirit to such a point that at last I was finally beginning to enjoy it.'

And I went on…

'If I'm brutally honest, I entered this course of therapy in a very negative frame of mind. My mind seemed set in stone that I simply wasn't willing to throw myself in, one hundred per cent. I now feel that in the past six weeks, although we have not solved all of my issues, I do think that I have made great progress as a result of seeing you. Oh, and as for today's session, I do think maybe it's time for you to do the talking and time for you to tell me how you think these sessions have gone.

'Am I right?' I joked.

'Indeed, Kelly, those random questions that I asked you on your first visit and earlier this session were assessment and analysis based questions,' she said. 'Each question was set as a point-scoring exercise, and with that in mind, on your first visit your total score was twenty-seven, which is quite high. Nevertheless, I am happy to inform you that your score today is a positively staggering two. This, of course, is a massive improvement and a resounding success. But although you have moved forward and things are a lot better, I must now tell you that over these past few weeks I have picked up on a couple of issues that I will be writing to your doctor about.

'Now, Kelly, please make an appointment with your GP for a week's time so that you can discuss the next step.'

* * *

So there I was, back on the phone booking an appointment to see my doctor. Back and forth, forward and back… It seemed one hell of a laborious process, a process that I honestly thought would be over and done with by now. Nevertheless, my appointment came round quickly, which was lucky really because it didn't leave me with any time to ponder. To be honest, I think I was still processing the previous six weeks' sessions in my head anyway – trying to analyse the outcome, seeing if I could add or apply anything that might at least be of some sort of benefit.

It was a morning appointment that I had with the doctor, which I was very pleased about, because it didn't allow me any time in the day to get myself into the state of nervous stress that I usually found myself in: forever overthinking certain scenarios, like what the results were going to show up, and what certain results would mean. Also, it didn't allow me time to maybe ask my friends a million and one questions in the hope of answers of a reassuring nature.

'Sit down, Kelly,' were the first words from the doctor. He carried on: 'So, I have received the therapist's report, and first and foremost, I would like to hear your feelings with regard to you starting with a form of antidepressant?'

I explained to the doctor that I had heard that antidepressants simply mask the problem and they don't actually solve anything. I also told him that in my opinion, I was not depressed at all, so why would I want to take antidepressants? We spoke about how they might work and what effects they could have in alleviating a number of issues, and for this reason, he highly recommended that I give them a try – just for a short term at first, maybe three to six months – and then I could come back and we could assess the results, positive or negative, and see what adjustments needed to be made.

The doctor also said that the therapist's report had recommended that I go and see a psychologist in the mental health department. I told him that in my view, when you say the word 'mental', it conjures up so many horrific images in my head – someone who is mad, a person that is out of control, a loose cannon, a volcano about to erupt, toys in the attic… crazy!

'There just seems to be an invisible label attached to the word "mental" – and it scares me,' I admitted.

The doctor reassured me about my fears surrounding the word 'mental' and told me that I wasn't 'mental', but I just needed to change my thought patterns and have a bit of professional help to overcome my issues. He said that he would refer me back to see a psychologist, but once again, I should prepare myself for at least a couple of months' waiting time. By that time the antidepressants would have had time to get into my system, and hopefully I would be feeling some real solid benefits. So, as requested, I began to take the antidepressants. Scott was worried that taking antidepressants would only mask the problem, and he worried that I would get hooked on them, creating yet another issue for me. However, I had to try.

But I did not feel that they were working, and as you've probably realised by now, I am very impatient and I wanted to see results immediately. All those meds seemed to do was suppress my appetite and make me even more moody. Any sort of positive emotion had been stripped from my body – I just felt numb and dead inside, like a zombie staring at the wall for hours on end.

'Oh, for f**k's sake, this is no good!' I thought to myself, so it was back to the doctor's once again.

At which point the doctor prescribed a new tablet. Of course I didn't have much faith in this one doing anything different. Nevertheless, I told myself, 'Kelly, give it a spin, girl. Try to be po-si-tiiiiive!' And through gritted teeth I soldiered on.

As I expected, this new antidepressant had exactly the same effect on me as the first, so I decided to stop taking it. Also, I decided that I wasn't going to go back to the doctor's to be used as a guinea pig anymore. I mean, what damage were these tablets doing to my body? I just wasn't prepared to stuff myself with these chemicals anymore. Meanwhile I hoped the appointment to see the psychologist would drop through my letter box a bit lively, because my head was telling me that the therapy with the psychologist was just what I needed to get better and that taking copious amounts of happy pills was a waste of time.

Anyway, I finally got my appointment through. This appointment was set for the very next Friday morning, at 9.30am, and as I do with every scenario in my life, I immediately began the inevitable process of overthinking it. The letter had stated that it was a straight two-hour-long assessment, so I immediately began looking for any given angle at my disposal, should I wish to get out of it double-quick. Now, let me see…

> 'I start my shift at school at twelve o'clock!'
> 'So if my appointment starts just slightly late, I can say I need to leave right away because I simply can't miss my work.'

I'm not really sure why I was looking for a get-out plan. Maybe it was down to nerves – the unknown, the dreaded thought of change. Anyway, the plan fell at the first hurdle because the psychologist called me into her office at bang on nine thirty. AAAARRRRGGGHHHHH!

So we sat down and she asked me why I thought I was there. I explained to her about my six sessions with the therapist and her recommendations etc., and so here I was in all my glory.

Of course, all of the above was obviously already in my notes, and she would have seen the referral report beforehand. Nevertheless, as is the way with many professional people, she let me rattle on. The only thing she did address from the report were the notes made with regard to my obsessive behaviour.

'We would like to assess you over the next few months,' she told me.

She also asked me many similar questions to the ones the therapist had asked. Like the film *Groundhog Day*, it seemed to me that we were revisiting the same old stuff that I'd been over before. I was beginning to get tired of this – I just couldn't see the point of it anymore. I wasn't getting any answers that justified these visits. For all intents and purposes, I was still the same troubled person as before.

One question I did keep asking was this:

'Do I have bipolar…?'

'No, Kelly, you do not have bipolar, and why do you keep asking me that question?' she said patiently.

'Well, I don't want bipolar,' I told her. 'But I do seem to have a lot of the same traits: I don't sleep; I start jobs, but I don't finish them before moving on to the next project; I'm constantly hyper, which is followed by fatigue, resulting in heavy spells in bed; and these, I am aware, are all major signs of someone with bipolar.'

The doctor went on to tell me that I was indeed correct in my assumption and that these were 'some' of the traits of bipolar, but not all of them. She went on to clarify that we were moving forward, that it takes time to make the right assessment and that it would be a little while longer before she would, or for that matter could, make an educated judgement. So, the months dragged on and on and on, and still no diagnosis.

I continued my journey back and forth to see the psychologist once a week, going over the same old stuff, and to be quite honest, there didn't seem to be a great deal of progress, hardly any benefit at all in my opinion. It seemed as though we just kept going over the same old set of scenarios week in, week out. In fact, I carried on seeing the psychologist for a whole two years. Then finally, one particular day, I went into the office and she sat me down.

'Kelly, I have come to my conclusion,' she announced.

At which point a funny feeling came over me. In a way, I was shocked – I was just going along with the sessions, but now, finally, I had something to work on. All these thoughts were going through my head:

'Am I mad?'
'Am I abnormal?'
'What the f**k is wrong with me?'

Immediately, I sat bolt upright. I could feel the intensity of my eyes burning into her, longing for some verification, some kind of answer. The anticipation was killing me inside.

'Well, first and foremost, I am sorry it has taken so long to come up with my conclusion, but I had to be sure. Getting to know you and the way in which your mind works a whole lot more, I also needed to rule out certain traits within your personality that were leaving me with unanswered questions in my head. Questions such as,

'"Is this a part of her mental instability, or is it simply Kelly's personality?"

'"Am I reading too much into certain parts of her mind and analysing them with nothing to substantiate my investigation?"

'And also, of course, '"Is everything Kelly's offloading to me her true feelings or simply a guise in order to get the job done quicker?"

'And all of the aforementioned has taken almost a period of two years to establish that my first thoughts, and indeed my final analysis, were correct.'

It was at this point that she diagnosed me with a condition known professionally as cyclothymia, a condition very similar to the more common condition known as bipolar. Similar to bipolar, it involves recurrent hypomanic (persistently elevated or expansive mood) and dysthymic (persistently mild depression) episodes, but it doesn't usually bring on full manic episodes nor full major depressive episodes.

I was advised that I should start medicating myself with lamotrigine, a mood stabiliser for those with my condition. Lamotrigine, as I have come to understand it, also works for people who suffer with epilepsy too, but for me it is supposed to level out my highs and lows, bringing them down to a more acceptable, or shall we say 'normal' level.

'For f**k's sake, I've never been normal! Ask my Scott...' I thought.

I was also told that failure to take my medication could result in my condition turning into full-blown bipolar.

There was another, very interesting piece of factual evidence that the psychologist educated me with, and that was that my condition was hereditary, and either my mum or dad could have suffered with either cyclothymia or bipolar too. And after the stories you have read here in my book, and the people reading this who were actually friends with my mum would agree, it certainly wouldn't have been Mum who would have suffered with any such condition. However, my dad was never tested or in fact diagnosed with either bipolar or cyclothymia, and in my view, he had all of the traits of a person suffering with either one of those conditions. He could also have been suffering with a form of OCD, although judging from the state of his car, I would have to disagree. Joking apart, OCD manifests itself in many different ways – an uncontrollable, repetitive obsession being one of them, which could be true for my dad. Well, anyway, without the slightest doubt, I believe that he had the same chemical imbalance in his brain as I do in mine, because we shared very similar ways, thoughts and actions.

You see, when I look back at the way my dad dealt with many situations, it's plain for me to see a likeness in the way that I too deal with my life experiences. Please let me explain how he and I would react in a similar way: we could be in a conversation with someone. Now any person without my condition would hear this conversation in a non-offensive manner, but I believe my dad and I would take it as a challenge, a dig or even a personal attack. Immediately, our backs would be up and we would both react in an extremely aggressive way, which seemed to be the only way our brains would tell us to respond in such a situation. Nevertheless, since being diagnosed with cyclothymia, I have tried hard to change the way I hear and the way I react to certain situations. As I mentioned earlier in this book, there is always a reason behind a person's actions.

Dad would often react to situations in a similar way

to how he would treat my mum at times, which was terrible. When you look at it a bit deeper, he didn't react this way because he was a bully, though. No, he had this chemical imbalance in his brain that told him how he should react. My dad had a condition that was never diagnosed, so how could he deal with it, if he never knew that he was suffering from it?

As for me, now that I have finally been diagnosed, I have at last been given the tools. I have gained a certain amount of knowledge that will indicate to me how I should deal with certain situations on a daily basis. And for this reason I now look at my dad and his behaviour in a completely and utterly different way. Instead of sometimes hating him and judging him, I now feel truly sorry for him. My poor dad, having to go through the whole of his life with a deeply troubled and somewhat damaged brain.

He must have hated the way he treated my mum – the love of his life – but he just didn't have the tools to change his behaviour. If I'm brutally honest, I'm a little ashamed to admit to the thoughts I once harboured towards my own dad. So, Dad, if you can see or at least hear me now, I do hope that you can find it in your heart to forgive me.

I would have loved to have had the chance to help my dad with his many issues in much the same way as

LIFE AFTER

I am trying to deal with my own life as I sit here today. I am trying to create a stable, caring and loving family life for my children and partner alike, and although it seems as though I am on the winning team, it isn't always sunshine and roses. The battle I fight appears on an almost daily basis, and it's a battle I simply cannot afford to take my eye off, not for a single, solitary second.

15

TODAY

Today, as we tiptoe ever closer to a conclusion to this story, I feel that it's only right to bring you up to speed with the true facts that I have kept to myself for the past forty years.

So, am I at peace with myself today? Well, the answer to that is a great big fat resounding NO! I honestly couldn't say that I am. As for the task I set myself, of working to become a better person... well, yes, I do think that I have finally conquered that battle. To be honest, though, I never actually believed that I was a bad person to start with – I'd just made some questionable decisions in the past. I have been working to become a more relaxed person, someone who assesses a situation, rather than jumping in feet first and judging it. I am today someone who can adapt and react to situations in a calmer manner, trying my hardest to react in a way that brings about the least amount of conflict. Today, I try and look at every person's point of view rather than jumping in feet first with my conclusion. I try to take a few steps back, take a few deep breaths and then reach a conclusion, leaving any kind of gut instinct at the door.

I am by no means perfect – I still have many moments when the irrational part of my brain kicks in and takes over with negative thoughts, bringing to the fore the red mist of Kelly McLean. I react and jump in with both feet. Nevertheless, these episodes are becoming less and less frequent, as I begin to learn more and more about myself. With my condition, I now know that I need to question myself first, taking a look at the initial thought that is forcing itself to the front of my head and questioning it. Every day, I try to think about my thought process, think hard about how and why, in the hope that this newfound technique helps me to react in the appropriate and correct way. Now that I have a diagnosis, I know that there is a reason for my thoughts and that I need to challenge them. I've bought books and done a lot of research outside of my therapy sessions, and always remind myself to take a breath first before I react to things.

Today, I spend a lot of time going over in my head: just who exactly was Kelly McLean growing up?

TODAY

Because today, the Kelly McLean I remember from my childhood is a total stranger to me. Today, in my forties and having been diagnosed with cyclothymia, I am truly beginning to learn just who I am – the Kelly McLean of the past would react to almost every situation in a very similar way to her dad.

As I take a virtual tour around my mind through my childhood, I would say that yes, I did react differently to most of the world. And my mum was indeed correct when she told a neighbour that her Kelly would be OK when she heard that I was fighting with a bunch of older girls – 'Yes, that's my Kelly. She's her father's daughter!'

See, mine and my dad's brains worked in exactly the same way: the two of us had a chemical imbalance in our brains, but unfortunately for Dad, his condition was never diagnosed. Fortunately for me though, I have now been diagnosed, although for the first forty years of my life, I was completely in the dark. My brain was in control of everything I did, torturing me and telling me what was right and wrong. At that time I too saw things a little boss-eyed, as my dad would say.

Today, in contrast to the first forty years of my life, there are two different people inside my head:

A normal, calm person

A good-natured and peaceful person

Yet also:

An aggressive, argumentative character

A person who jumps in, both feet first, and to hell with the consequences!

Sadly for me, and many people around me at that time, the latter was the person I became, the person who won each and every battle in her head, every last one of them. I must admit sometimes I enjoyed living life on the edge, being a little different to everyone else in the crowd, but over time living this way took its toll on me. There were times when I would lock myself away from the world, draw the curtains and not answer the phone, or even open the door. Days such as these could run into a whole week at times. I would get myself into such a state, and the feeling of loneliness would engulf me, the sadness would almost break me. The mind works in some very odd ways with mental instability – having feelings like these, yet all the while locking myself away from the very people who might have been able to comfort me.

As a child, I remember my dad going back to bed during the day. He would always say, 'Kelly, don't tell anyone about Daddy going to bed in the daytime,' but at such a young age, I really couldn't understand his reasons for doing this. Dad never locked himself away for days on end in the same way as me, but most days he would go back to bed for a couple of hours. As an adult, and with the same sort of brain as my dad, it is now a lot clearer to me why he did this, and that reason is… peace!

I too have a similar routine – I often take a couple of hours' nap to rest my nervous system. You see, when you are sleeping, your mind is at rest and you feel totally serene. Nevertheless, momentarily as I wake, my mind starts to race again, overthinking everything. Was this the same for my dad? Well, I believe so, but unfortunately, I will never be 100 per cent sure.

I feel sad knowing that my dad had to suffer, that he was never gifted with the tools to lead a normal life. Dad never had the opportunity of a little peace in his head; all of the things that he went through, with the knowledge available today, could have been so very different. But I like to think that he would at least be at peace in the knowledge that his daughter finally found the right tools, and through this, was given the opportunity to change her life. I now know that it's down to me, and the artillery I have, to fight these demons and live the kind of life that the new Kelly McLean chooses to live.

Losing my mum and dad took a lot out of me and if it wasn't for my twin daughters, Ruby and Prudence, I honestly believe that I wouldn't be sitting here today. As I have said earlier, after losing Dad, I slipped into a deep depression – I simply couldn't see a way out, my mind was full to bursting with negative thoughts. I was sinking deeper and deeper. So very deep, in fact, that just six months later, I tried to take my own life…

The pain and sadness I was suffering was too much for me to bear – I didn't want to live this way anymore, I couldn't see an end to this depression. Through sheer panic I took out a pen and some paper, and wrote two letters: one to my mum and the other to my brother, Jamie. With trembling hands, I wrote:

To Mum/Jamie
I truly love you more than life it self.
And I am deeply sorry for what I am about to do.
But you see, life has become far too painfull
    for me,
And way too complicated for my brain to
    understand.
The pain that I have inside of me after looseing
daddy, is just to much for me to bare.
I am truly sorry…
Yours
Kelly xxx

TODAY

I left the notes beside me on the bed, then lay myself back down and began popping handful after handful of pills. A short while later, unbeknown to me, I dozed off. I remember stirring in my sleep. I'm not exactly sure what it was that woke me. Still jaded and confused, I tried to lift my head off the pillow and ease myself out of bed, although I didn't get very far before collapsing in a heap on the floor. My head wasn't with it, yet I remember plain as day, the promising thought rushing through my still-weary head…

'Wow, the tablets are working! I'll be free from this pain very soon. No more hurting, no more darkness.'

By and large, people say that suicide is a coward's way out. What about the people left behind to deal with the aftermath – the children, the family and friends all left grieving in the dark, with no rhyme or reason as to why that person has sunk to such a disturbing level? Well, my answer is plain and simple: suicide occurs as a last resort, the final step into a gaping hole, a dark void of nothingness. Nevertheless, it's an end, an end to all of the pain. You see, the suicidal person has sunk to such a low point in their life that they believe there are just no other options open to them, no other pathways of relief from all the sadness. Alone they stand, ready to jump into a neverending pit of destruction. Suicide, today, is indeed their only saviour, or so they believe.

So, there I was, lying on my bedroom floor, unconscious. I hadn't realised to what extent my mum was concerned about my health. She tried to phone me many times, and when that failed, she contacted my friends to find out if anybody had seen me. But these attempts all fell on stony ground – there was simply no sign of me anywhere. At that point she quickly realised that something was wrong and immediately drove round to my flat to check up on me.

At that time in my life, I lived in a house that had been converted into two flats. My flat was on the ground floor; our two flats shared the front door. There was a corridor leading to the first-floor flat and my front door was at the bottom of the stairs leading to it. You could quite literally peek through the letter box and see into my bedroom.

Moments later, Mum arrived at the flats. Luckily, the communal door was open – it was always left open during the day. The tenant who lived upstairs would be constantly in and out, and every time he closed the front door, my flat would shake. This often drove me wild and so I had asked him to leave it open. Bang, bang, bang! I could hear the door. Not getting an answer, my mum bent down and looked through the letter box straight into my bedroom. She could see that I was sprawled out on the floor. In a state of panic, she immediately started to shout and bang on the door. In all of the commotion I came to and somehow managed to crawl to the door and open it.

Mum reached down, swung her arms around me and through her tears asked me what had happened. I noticed that she glanced over and spotted the empty bottle of tablets on the bed and also the letters that I had written earlier. At this she completely broke down. She could not understand why I had tried to do such a desperate thing – 'Kelly, darling, you have so much to live for!' she gasped. And how right she was.

At that moment in time, suicide seemed the only option left open to me, but lo and behold, of course there was another way – I just had to find the fight within me to get myself through it. If I had died that day, depression would have won. I would have lost my mum and she would have lost her one and only daughter. Like a lightbulb switching on in my head, an epiphany came over me: 'She's right, I'm just a young woman. I can get through this, I can beat it once and for all. This surely has to be the final straw…'

With that, my mum started to throw a million questions at me. Not being altogether with it, I said, 'Mum, I can't deal with this barrage of questions right now. Look, I know I was stupid and I promise you that I will not do anything like this ever again.'

But being the cunning person that I was, I knew that I would just paper over the cracks. I would simply cast the questions aside that she had thrown at me and never address a single one of them. I had no intention of speaking to her about my pain. Instead, I decided to do what I have always done throughout my life and that was to put it to the back of my mind and make out none of it had ever happened. Now that, my dearest friends, truly is the coward's way out – I should have just dealt with the problems there and then.

There are many more ways that my dad and I were very similar. Oh, he never tried to commit suicide – well, not to my knowledge anyway – but he did have very low points in his life, devastating low points that he never shared with anyone outside of his immediate family. As I have mentioned earlier, Dad and I dealt with many situations in a very similar way, and this I mostly put down to cyclothmia, the debilitating condition that I have and a condition that I truly believe my Dad was suffering with too.

However, not all of our mindset is just down to cyclothmia. As most of you will know, my dad had an abusive upbringing. As I have said earlier, he was physically and mentally abused by his stepfather. My upbringing was never physical, but living with my dad was mentally challenging at times.

While writing this book, I have gained a great deal of knowledge with regard to how we as human beings work. Many of us keep secrets from one another, for if we share certain feelings, beliefs and thoughts, we are very quickly labelled, judged shamefully and negatively categorised as a certain 'type'. Over time, the sh*t finally sticks, and no matter how hard you work to try and change people's opinions of you, many people are just not willing to allow you to change the given stereotype.

I am the world's worst at storing these kind of thoughts and emotions in the back of my head, never one to share with anyone the pain and the torture that I have to deal with on a daily basis. Yet with the tools I have now for dealing with things, I know that if you are able to open up and share some of those thoughts and emotions, it might halve the pain you are feeling, and in most cases help in your road to recovery.

The alarming event that I am about to share with you was in my head, under lock and key, and it was going to my grave with me – although I think in sharing it with you, I feel safe in the knowledge that none of you will judge me, and that quite possibly this could aid in my recovery. This single harmful event has taken me almost forty years to share with anyone. I hope that by opening up to you in this very public way, this could stop what happened to me happening to anybody else reading this. But if any of you out there are ever faced with such a thing, please do not be frightened to speak out. I beg of you not to live in fear of being called a liar. Just open up and tell the truth, and believe me, your cry for help will be heard by someone.

Right, count to ten, Kelly, and practise what you have just this second preached. OK, there's no easy way of saying this, so I'm just going to come out with it… As a child I was sexually abused by a neighbour. I used to play with this girl, and on this particular day, we were playing in her bedroom. Then all of a sudden my friend's older sister entered the room: she wanted to play a game that we used to play in the seventies called Doctors and Nurses. Anyone my age and above will have played this game, and quite innocently too. It was just that – a game.

The game would consist of one of you (me in this instance) being the patient, and the other would play the role of the nurse or the doctor, whichever suited. My role was to lie on the bed as she (the older sister) operated on me. At this point in the game she began to touch me in my private area. Being just five years old, I didn't know that this was wrong. Nevertheless,

I do remember thinking something wasn't quite right. This scenario happened a couple of times, and by the time we had reached the second game, I knew that this definitely was not right.

'My mummy doesn't touch me in my private area, so what gives this girl the right to do it to me?' I remember thinking to myself.

A little confused, but ultimately frightened, I hurried home. When I arrived home, I decided not to tell my mum and dad. Why? I hear you ask. Well, at that tender age I couldn't really say.

Was I worried that they wouldn't believe me?

Did I think maybe I would be told off?

Or, and this is most definitely the reason: was I worried about how my dad would react?

I think I can safely say that yes, it was most certainly that.

Of course I, and I'm guessing a great many of you who are reading this right now, know exactly how my dad would have reacted. He would have reacted in the only way that he knew how. And there's not a single doubt in my mind that in his rage he would have flown from our house and killed the father of the girl who had sexually abused me.

In opening up to my dad about this horrible event, I would have altered the course of both our lives forever.

Oh yes, I would not have had to carry this dark secret with me for almost forty years, that's a given. But it would have changed The Guv'nor's life in a split second, because my dad, Lenny McLean, would have been serving a life sentence for murder.

So, was I right in not telling my mum and dad about it? Well, I certainly didn't feel that I had any other options open to me. I was only five years old, a child. I didn't have the first clue what was the best thing to do. The only control I did have was to put it to the back of my head, to deal with another day. And this is where it all began, a dark secret locked away in an innocent little five-year-old girl's head. For forty years I have kept that secret: embarrassed, ashamed, yet most of all living with the agonising feeling of regret that I never told my parents. Although I did come close to it one day when my mum was dying of cancer and we were alone on her bed. Out of the blue, she asked me if there was anything that I wanted her to know, or was there anything I wanted to say to her.

I looked into her eyes and thought to myself, 'How can I tell her about the abuse? What would I gain from telling her? All it will do is break her heart.' Finding out that I had never confided in her, and that her only daughter had carried this terrible secret alone through life for so many years, would only upset her. So I simply smiled, looked my dear mum in the eye and said, 'Mum, you were, are, and will always be the very best mum in the world.' And for me, that was all she needed to hear.

So, here I am in my present life: January 2018. I'm about to go and ask my GP to refer me for another course of therapy. The big difference this time though is that I can go in there 100 per cent free, with nothing left in my closet, no stone unturned. I am now ready to make the very best of my life. Not only for me, but for my precious children, Prudence and Ruby, and my partner and rock, Scott.

Life, as we all know, can be tough, and at times it can deal you some very bad cards. Living a normal life can sometimes be an arduous task, but I have learned that it is the way in which we deal with it that eventually sees us rewarded with some peace of mind.

I need to try and learn to forgive, even though I may not be able to forget. I must try to understand that human beings do certain things for certain reasons, and whether I see those reasons as good or bad, and I may not agree with them, I have to let them get on with it, because it is their choice. And I, Kelly McLean, no matter how strong my will, cannot, and will not, ever be able to change that.

DEDICATIONS

JOHN 'THE NECK' HOUCHIN

My name is John Houchin. I was very good pals with Lenny McLean for about thirteen years. I was a relatively young yet seasoned minder, or a man that was penned in Lenny's little black book under the words, 'muscle for hire'. Well, whichever way we chose to describe our union, Len took me under his wing and put me to work on his finely tuned 'firm'.

Len's firm, a gladiatorial bunch to say the least, were handpicked by The Guv'nor himself. And let me tell you this, he had wrapped around him the finest bunch of tasty bouncers, enforcers and money-getters you could ever wish to meet, or for that matter NEVER WISH TO MEET if indeed you were on the wrong side of them!

Although I feel it is a great honour to be asked by Len's only daughter, Kelly McLean, to say a few words in dedication to my dear friend Lenny, it is for me a very emotional experience. You see, I and another of Lenny's dear friends and work colleagues, Al Crossley, were the two men Lenny asked to look after him at his very last book signing at Dillons bookstore in Oxford Street. And although it was a very proud time for all of us involved, we – and of course Len – knew that for him the end was close. And as I recall my thoughts to my friend Lee Wortley, it is in fact bringing back all kinds of memories, happy and sad. So let's just concentrate on the happy ones!

Len and his precious little family were like a second family to me. His wife Valerie shared the same name as my very own mum and was every bit as nurturing. Len's children, Kelly and Jamie, were the apple of his eye and he never stopped talking about them. And that brings me on to my friend Len.

Len was the best friend a man could ever wish to have, and that for me could never be contested. Being fifteen years my senior, he was something of a father figure to me, and I looked up to him in the same way that I did my very own father. Lenny McLean was staunch, respectful, loyal to a fault, and believe it or not, one of the humblest men I have ever known. He was undeniably one of the greatest fist fighters I have ever seen in action, and when Len went to work (had to use his muscle), he made light work of any given situation, no matter how terrifying. If Len was your pal, then take it from me, your back was well and truly covered. I miss him each and every day. However, his legacy being kept alive to the masses across each and every platform in some way makes me feel like he is still around.

Bless you, my friend. Your friendship helped me in more ways than you ever knew.

Yours,

John 'The Neck'

NEIL BARR
Fanatical follower of The Guv'nor

Before I write my dedication to Lenny, I would like to say a massive thank you to Kelly for our friendship and for affording me the opportunity to say a little something in this book about one of my very few idols. We met a few years ago through Kelly's awesome site on Facebook, which is dedicated to her dad, and our friendship has grown and continues to grow.

She is an absolute diamond of a lass – straightforward,

genuine, honest and most definitely salt of the earth and 'what you see is what you get'. A rarity in this day and age, and someone I'm proud to call my friend. One of the things I love about Kelly is that every year, on 9 April, without fail, she'll send me a voice message and a Gif (animated image) wishing me and her dad a happy joint birthday and to make sure I have a drink for us both – and every year, without fail, I'll send her a voice message back the next morning, whingeing about how hungover and rank I feel. In true Kelly style, she takes the p*ss and gets a smile out of my rough miserable chops. Even when my mam died in August 2016, she was there giving me support through talking and messages and the likes. Thank you for always being there, Kelly. You're an absolute star and I know your dad is looking down on you and smiling with great love and pride.

I have been a fan of Lenny McLean since around 1999. I had seen the odd clip of his monumental fights and then I saw him in *Lock, Stock and Two Smoking Barrels*. It wasn't until a year or so later, when I read his autobiography, that I actually realised he was the guy I had seen in those fighting clips a few years previously. That's when my interest in this enigma of a man became almost non-stop.

The more I read and researched about The Guv'nor,

the more I saw just how similar our lives were. We were even born on the same day, only twenty-seven years apart. At the time of reading his book, I was falling severely off-track – I was letting all of the hatred and anger I had inside of me win. All that sh*t I went through as a kid very nearly turned me into a bad person, who didn't care because f**k you, world, you've been bad to me – so I'm comin' at you ten-fold!

We had scarily similar childhoods – full of anger, aggression, and to put it mildly, being mistreated by the very ones who were meant to 'care' for us. Physical beatings and mental torture that most others, thankfully, cannot comprehend!

When I read his book, I couldn't believe how similar we were in our ways: our views, morals and principles; our respect for only those who deserve it; our loving, caring, nurturing natures, always looking out for those weaker than us; and above all, our hatred for bullies. I always had those qualities, but somewhere along the line I nearly forgot until Lenny got a grip of me through his book.

Like Lenny, I used to bully the bullies. Anyone picking on somebody smaller or weaker than them or caught taking advantage of someone, BEWARE!

We're both fighters, but in different ways. Big Lenny channelled his hatred, anger and aggression in the ring through unlicensed boxing and bare-knuckle fighting and became the true champion, whereas I joined the army at the age of seventeen to try and channel mine, but also, I was still good at knocking out the wrongdoers of this world! Incidentally, nowhere near as good as Lenny – I WISH! Ha ha!

I can honestly say that every single time I was steering off-track or life was getting on top of me, or even when I was facing adverse circumstances, all I had to do was pick up that book and have a read, and somewhere in those pages there was always a solution to my problem, or I would sit and think, 'What would Lenny do?' I can cast-iron guarantee that I always found a positive message in his words and used it to do good rather than bad – and it's partly down to you, Lenny, that I am the man I am today. I wish you were here for me to thank you in person, because I owe you a massive debt of gratitude for the help and guidance you have unknowingly given me.

Forever in my heart and thoughts, RIP, Big Man! Will hopefully meet you when it's my turn... until then, rest easy, Lenny 'The Guv'nor' McLean.

DEDICATIONS

NATHAN LOWE

My name is Nathan, or 'Mr Lowe' to any of the pupils who reside under the roof of our school – Flitch Green Academy. Within these walls, I take up the role of principal, a position that I hold very close to my heart. Our academy houses the finest pupils and staff members alike, the most truly dedicated bunch that you could ever wish to meet, and Kelly plays a crucial part in her role as after-school co-ordinator, a position she so passionately shoulders.

Kelly and I first met in one of our school corridors, a veritable chit-chat meeting place for staff and pupils alike. Now Kelly is somewhat of a chatterbox, as I'm sure her friends and indeed her very own school teachers would agree, although I must confess that she is a chatterbox with a story to tell at any given moment. If I'm to be quite honest, most of her stories quite literally captivated me, as I am sure they will have captivated you too as you've read through the pages of this fantastic book.

This book is a tribute to Kelly's late father, Lenny McLean – a man of whom I had heard, but really knew nothing about. Nevertheless, what I will say is that it is very clear for me to see that this lady is a carbon copy of her father in every distinguishable way, and this is a conclusion that I have drawn from the smallest amount of detail that I found. Kelly, for me, is quick-witted like her late father, and also a truly kind and giving person.

I first met Kelly when she joined our team of staff in 2009, and it was clear she had a real passion for working with children. She enjoys a chat each evening and is always ready to share one of her stories… or two! Often, her stories are about her late father, Lenny McLean. It's a real pleasure to work with Kelly and see the enthusiasm and energy she brings to her role each evening.

RACHEL REBEHKA HALLIWELL
Close friend of the McLeans

In 1992, I got a job in London and moved down there with the help of a friend who had connections in the London underworld. On arrival, I was introduced to a fella called Eddie, who had a carpet shop down the Roman Road in the East End of London, and soon after, I was introduced to Kelly McLean.

At that time, Lenny had The Guv'ner's pub, and Len's daughter, Kelly McLean, was running it for her dad; coincidentally, at that precise time, she was in need of staff. Well, I visited the pub on a number of occasions, and in no time at all, I had moved in with Kelly and we became the very best of friends. Now over the next few months, while at the pub, I visited Lenny and Val's house in Bexleyheath with Kelly, and once The Guv'ner's pub came to an end, I moved in to 13 Strahan Road with Lenny and Val, who became like second parents to me.

Valerie was the ever-doting mother hen with a heart of solid gold; she treated me like one of her own and that I will never forget. Leaving all of the aggressive side of Lenny to one side, to me he was like a big cuddly bear and one of the funniest and most quick-witted men I have ever had the pleasure of knowing.

One night when we were sat in the lounge, Len was watching *This Is Your Life*, and I said to him, 'Here, Len, you ought to go on this programme,' and he replied, 'Oh yeah, I can just see it now, Rachel. That Eamonn Andrews fella would go, "Well, Lenny, here's a fella you haven't seen for a great number of years, but he never forgot the day when you smashed his f**king head in! Lenny, would you please welcome onto the stage…"' Giggling, he carried on with, 'Oh yes, babe, I can just see it now! Ha, ha, ha,' and we both laughed like schoolkids in school assembly.

Like I said previously, Lenny had The Guv'ner's pub and Kel and I were living upstairs. We would come down into the pub every time. It didn't matter what events were going on, we would be down there. Anyway, this one night it was stripper night, so obviously the pair of us were down in the bar, having a laugh. Well, one of these strippers (a well-known celebrity) was all over me like a rash – he wouldn't leave me alone, he couldn't get enough of me. So anyway, Lenny found out about it, and the next day he came home from the gym (Slim Jim's in Greenwich, for the record) and said to me, 'Right, I've had a few words with this stripper fella and he won't be trying any of that sh*t again. Now I ain't having it, Rachel, a f**king fella like that wrapping himself around the likes of you. Well, it ain't happening!'

Well, the next time I bumped into this fella, in a very hangdog manner he said to me, 'Hey Rachel, you live with Lenny McLean, don't you?' to which I replied rather sternly, 'Yes, I do!' And that was the end of that little saga.

Lenny, Val and my dear friend Kelly were always there for me and I love the very bones of them. Kelly and I have continued to be the greatest of friends and her beautiful twins are a credit to her and Scott. Lenny and Val would be so proud of you, Kelly; this book is the final part of the Lenny McLean jigsaw and a true testament to your dad's legacy.

I will never forget Lenny and Valerie McLean. They were there for me every step of the way, and I love and miss them so very dearly.

Your forever friend,

Rachel

HENRY SIMPSON

Over a relatively short period of time, I have become very fond of my dear friend Lenny McLean's one and only beautiful daughter, Kelly Valerie McLean, so when I was kindly asked by her to write a dedication for her book, I was absolutely bowled over to say the least, and indeed considered it to be a real privilege.

Kelly can write about her father, the man no one else living now could have truly known; only she can inform us of the man behind the McLean family door, and the ways in which he behaved away from the often harsh and sometimes damning spotlight.

Now a little about myself and just how I got together with this man who became such a legend. When the late Bert Rossi asked me to deliver his red letters (collector debts), I needed a bag man (a hard man hired to carry the cash). Having met Lenny 'Boy' McLean some time earlier, equipped as he was with that no-nonsense approach, which immediately impressed me, he was the only man for the job. However, once I had explained to Len how much he could expect to earn from this little bit of moonlighting, it became immediately apparent that I had in fact made a mistake, and a mistake that could turn out to be to my very own expense. I told him not only did the job come with a healthy pay packet, but also with a 10 per cent commision and expenses to boot.

'What's them?' he asked.

'Food and drink, Lenny!' I promptly answered, being in the dark to the fact that three sausage sandwiches, three teas, a giant cream bun and a drink to take away was just the very start. And with Lenny's newfound invisible VIP badge, Mr McLean soon had a list of his favourite cafés to stop at along the way, and I might add he ate very well at each and every last one of them.

'OK, H!' Len said. 'Let's give this little number a go...'

So, we collected mostly from very well-off people who had incurred hefty gambling debts, etc. We never went for the poor blokes trying to earn a crust, because Lenny, or for that matter myself too in fact, would never have taken on such deplorable or shameful

DEDICATIONS

work. Some of these wealthy debtors had their own staff, which they used to keep us out. So, Lenny and I would sometimes have to fight our way in, and even on the odd occasion fight our way out, if the job was a little stronger. Nevertheless, whatever came our way, I was never at all concerned, because I had Lenny McLean in front of me, and for me that was guarantee enough that I would make it home safe to my bed on that particular night.

My friend Lenny was unstoppable and indestructible. No matter how big or small, or how many stood in our way, he would roll them like pins in an alley and we would always succeed in being paid. Once we had the money and had earned our pay, Len would say, 'How about stopping on the way back for something to eat, H?' As time goes by, I think back to those days with a smile, because we had some great times together, and even more great laughs, and we always managed to earn a good few bob into the bargain too.

If I had to use a couple of words to describe my mate Lenny, they would be as follows… 'the best'!

Lenny was the best at collecting from the uncollectable… the best street fighter… the best doorman… with the best team at his disposal… the best minder…. and before he was sadly taken away

261

from us, he was well on his way to becoming one of the best actors of his kind as well.

Now, if Lenny was around today, he would be so proud of his daughter Kelly for producing this book. But wait, there is a kicker: if Lenny could read these thoughts of mine right now, that man would once again be chasing me around my car to give my poor old head a damn good squeeze...

But all jokes aside, if you can see these words, Lenny, I miss you, my friend, with every day that passes.

God bless,

Henry Simpson

CLARE BROWN
Friend to Kelly

I have known Kelly for about six years now; our kids went to the same school. In that time I have learnt a lot about her. If I was asked to sum her up in a few words, they would be crazy, funny, one hundred-mile-an hour, loud, but most of all, very honourable, honest, caring, with a big heart, and although to everyone she can seem to be the life and soul of it all, deep down she is very sensitive and can hurt easily.

We don't see much of each other, but I know if I

needed anything then I would only have to ask. She is a good encourager – with her help I managed my first mini triathlon a couple of years ago. She is a brilliant hairdresser. (But you have to keep the evening free as you will be there a while due to her being a perfectionist and liking a chat!) There's no end to her talents: she is always looking for her next project, from decorating the house to crocheting hats, the list is endless! Kelly will have a go at just about anything.

On a more serious note, she misses her mum and dad dearly, and writing this book and playing an active role in her dad's website on Facebook has enabled her to keep their memories alive. It's been a huge comfort to her to share her precious memories with everyone.

Kelly, your mum and dad would be so proud of the woman you are, and what you have achieved so far. I look forward to many more years of your friendship and seeing you achieve your dreams.

Lots of love,

Clare xxx

STEPHANIE POUND

We lived next door to Lenny, Val, Kelly and Jamie for the first nine years of my life. I remember every Friday at teatime, Lenny would call me and my sister for a tea party with Kelly and Jamie, as we were all good friends. We always had custard creams – Lenny's favourite. He would chase us all around, pretending to be a monster trying to steal the custard creams, laughing his head off. I have good memories of a man everyone saw as the Guv'nor, but who I saw as a loving dad, who loved his kids and always made us a part of that family.

KATI ALCOCK
Friend to Kelly

I have got to know Kelly over the past few years and we have developed a wonderful friendship. I first met her when my daughter Chloe became best friends with Kelly's daughters, Prudence and Ruby. The girls didn't know it at the time but they were at pre-school together and I often saw Kelly with the girls in our local park. Once my daughter started at the primary school, she became best friends with Prudence and they became pretty much inseparable over the years.

During this time I have been really fortunate to get to know Kelly and feel very lucky to be able to count her as a friend. She has welcomed Chloe into her family, and there is always an open door there for Chloe if she wants to go round. Chloe has been on holiday with Kelly, Scott and the girls, and it is so evident that Kelly can't do enough for her children – they really are her world.

I was diagnosed with breast cancer nine months ago, and during that time my friendship with Kelly has strengthened further. She's been there for me during every stage of the treatment, looked after my son Joshua, as well as Chloe, when I have felt sick and even force-fed me jacket potato straight after my surgery! She's had the children overnight, so that my husband and I were able to enjoy some time together and a bit of normality amidst the chaos of chemotherapy and surgery. Kelly's personal experiences of cancer with both her Dad and Mum means that she has really been able to empathise with me and help me get through the last few months.

I look forward to many more years of friendship.

AFTERWORD
BY KAREN LATIMER

A memory from Karen Latimer, my lifelong friend, who Mum and Dad loved like another daughter.

From the age of fourteen, I have been part of the McLean family. I was friends with Jamie, and then as I got closer to the family, Kelly and I became very good friends. Then, as time went on, I was like part of the furniture. Val and Lenny loved me like one of their own children, and I loved them like another set of parents. Lenny was like a big kid – always playing pranks, and mainly on me, I might add. One story comes to mind…

One Saturday, I called up for Kelly and Lenny shouted out, 'Kelly, Karen's here!' 'Come up, babe,' he said, 'Kelly's doing her hair.' I went up to find Val and Kelly out. Lenny put the double-bolt on the door to keep me in and said, 'Fell for it, dozy! Put the kettle on then, make your Uncle Len a cuppa.' Val used to tell him off, and Lenny would be behind her back, pulling faces and clenching his fist at me, saying, 'She don't mind, Val. Do you, babe?' I had no choice – ha, ha, ha!

The day Lenny passed away was devastating. We were all with him and he was strong to the very end. On the day of the funeral my flowers were placed at the back of the coffin – I got Lenny the double heart. Val said, 'Put Karen's flowers close to Lenny, because if Len had his way, that's where Karen would be sitting, right next to him.'

I still miss Lenny to this day and always will; he was such an amazing character. Then to our shock horror, within a few years Val became ill. My, that was heart-wrenching! It tore my life apart. It still hurts to talk about her. My heart still aches and it always will. My Valsey (that's what I called her), she was one of the most kind, most beautiful ladies you could ever wish to meet, with a heart to match. Her smile, her voice… in addition, her love, will stay with me forever. I will never get over losing her; losing them both was devastating, but they will always live on through us.

Kelly's two daughters, Prudence and Ruby, love

listening to our stories. In the eighteen months they had with Val, she packed in lots of memories. She doted on the girls; she absolutely loved them and was so upset that she was not going to see them grow up. Val made me promise I would love and be there for the girls as she would have been. That was an easy promise to make: I love Prudence and Ruby with all my heart, and now the girls are growing up, Kelly and I build their memories so Val and Lenny live on through them. Kelly has been to hell and back, losing both parents and facing her own insecurities, but she has come through it.

She is a marvellous mum, and I am proud of her.

Your dear friend,

Karen

ACKNOWLEDGEMENTS

I dedicate my book to my beautiful mum. My mum is my root, my foundation. She planted the seed that I base my life on. For as long as I can remember, you were always by my side to help and give me support and confidence. You were always the person I looked up to, you were always so strong, so sensitive, and so beautiful inside and out. Mum, if I had to choose between loving you and breathing, I would use my last breath to tell you 'I love you'. Love you always and forever.

Scott, you are my friend, my partner, but most of all you are my wall. Without you there, I would fall down. I love how you take care of me and how you keep working to be a better man, even on days I fail to be a better woman. Love you always.

To my beautiful girls, Prudence and Ruby. If I could only give you one thing in this life, I would give you the ability to see yourselves how I see you every single day. Perhaps then you would be able to understand just how special you are to me. Always believe in yourself, go on adventures, have fun and always be happy, treasure tiny miracles, and embrace life. Reach for the stars. Always remember you are my reason for living. Love you always and forever.

Karen, in life we don't meet people by accident. They are meant to cross our path for a reason. You are my best friend, my soulmate, my sister, and I couldn't imagine my life without you. In a sea of people, my eyes will always search for you.